MOM'S TURN

A Journal for the First Year of Motherhood and Stories for Staying Empowered

ISBN 978-1-7323940-0-1

e-ISBN 978-1-7323940-1-8

Library of Congress Control Number: 2018908356

Printed in Canada

FIRST CHOICE BOOKS

www.firstchoicebooks.ca

Victoria, BC

First Edition September 2018

Little Cow Books

Author Contact Email: Jennika.Ingram@gmail.com

Social Media:

Twitter: @MomsTurnJournal

Instagram: MomsTurnJournal

Facebook: www.facebook.com/AuthorJennikaIngram/

Website: https://jennikaingram.wixsite.com/mysite

Contents

For Callam

INTRODUCTION

"When we first had the baby I woke up to all this crying every night. Finally I had to tell my baby's daddy to go sleep in the other room."

The arrival of a new baby can eclipse every aspect of life, particularly if you are a first-time mother. This book will guide you through challenges that might come up and enable you to find solutions to push you through and help you feel empowered and upbeat.

Mom's Turn is a book where you can record your journey, separately from your baby's journey. It can be your secret mom's journal for all of your ups and downs; you may find you go from one emotion to another in the span of a few minutes. This book aims to be:

- ✾ A blueprint to chart your personal experiences during this special year
- ✾ A journal for your most precious moments and those when you wonder how you got here
- ✾ An opportunity to brainstorm and overcome personal challenges
- ✾ A glimpse at how other mothers in North America are reacting to the first year
- ✾ A place to take a few minutes to laugh, reflect, learn and record your thoughts
- ✾ It's a coloring book! So you can really make it your own!

In an effort to unite the universal feelings of motherhood many women share, *Mom's Turn* has incorporated the voices of real moms across North America: from the United States and Canada, from the East Coast to the West Coast. I interviewed married and single moms, and some mothers who were in the midst of a separation. I've included a range of ages, from moms who started their families as young as 21 or as old as 47. I added my own two cents—I was in my twenties when I became a mom. I have attempted to include a diverse group of mothers from a variety of backgrounds, ethnicities, lifestyles, and perspectives. I talked to moms who felt challenged and mothers who were simply grateful to be fulfilling a lifelong dream. In all of their stories, I focused on the silver linings that came out of their experiences and I shared how they were able to be resourceful and create positive outcomes. May their journeys will inspire and support you as you travel this always changing territory of motherhood.

How to use this book: It is a baby book for moms. This book can be used as a journal and the white space under the writing prompts can be used as a place to write your thoughts. There are also lines to add your own stories, as well as white space to write anything you want, even your endless "to do" list! You can start at the beginning of the journal or read in any order you choose.

Coloring Book, Charts, and Envelopes: The panels on the sides and in the opening of each chapter are there for you to color. If your child is lying asleep on your chest, or you are too tired to read, you may want to have the meditative option to zone out and color. In the front of the book, there's space to double-side tape or glue in envelopes, if you want to save a keepsake or flash drive in the book. At the back, you will find charts to fill in as events happen during the year. The cover is spill-resistant so feel free to take it with you on your baby outings!

Facts, Tips, and Jokes: I tried to collect facts and tips to help with baby care and mommy care to make things a little easier for mothers during this important first year. Any humor or quote not attributed is my (the author's) own content.

Month in Review, and My Story: At the end of each month, I share my story, recap with questions what you might have learned, suggest a treat for you, and share a few principles I learned as a mother.

Editorial Style: I chose to do the book in the Chicago Manual of Style; however, I deviated from the rules in a few places. I decided not to indent in the Bibliography due to page costs. I also chose to use the % sign and to add character names to some of the attributions for readability and relatability.

CHAPTER ONE

Imagining Baby

Family Photographs

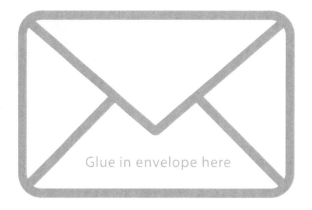

Glue in envelope here

A pocket for flash drives or memory sticks.

Year __ __ __ __

Envelope for Your First Gray Hairs

Glue in envelope here

BC: Before Child

"The reason most people have kids is because they get pregnant."

Barbara Kingsolver, *The Bean Trees*

When I picture being a mom, this is how I imagine my life will be...

My child will probably turn out to be...

One thing I want to remind myself to teach my child is...

The people who were supportive during my pregnancy were...

If you wanna be negative and say who was conspicuously absent I'm not going to stop you, but best to move forward with your cup half full... ;)

Tip: Don't be disappointed if your child doesn't arrive on time. Only 5% of all births arrive on the due date!

My baby arrived _____ days before/after/on time for (circle) the due date.

Checklist Pre-Baby

- ☐ **The car ride home.** Is the gas tank full? Car seat ready? Hurray for self-driving cars; one day parents will have the option of getting some shut-eye on the way home.

- ☐ **Consider your social media options.** Do you want to buy domain names, or create a newborn Facebook page or any other social media for your baby? Instagram, Pinterest, Twitter handles, blog, etc. You might consider joining Snapchat or Facebook Live to capture your day-to-day video moments for your family and friends. Unless of course you're already famous and trying to hide your baby's image from the world. ;)

- ☐ **Establish a list of places you can comfortably take a newborn.** Some examples include parks and playgrounds, the beach, child-friendly coffee shops and restaurants, drive-throughs, nearby libraries and story times, an area set apart for kids in museums, Gymboree classes, Ikea babysitting, empty movie theaters, the gym, swimming pools with wading pools. Weather permitting, you could head to a restaurant patio and have some friends join you.

"If I was going to re-think anything, I would take my time deciding how my lifestyle matches my needs for a certain type of car seat or stroller. My UPPAbaby® Vista stroller is awesome because I can fit three bags of groceries in the bottom, but if a mom doesn't plan on walking as much they probably wouldn't need to spend so much on a stroller."

Angie, *age 27*

❑ **Consider any baby gear you would like to purchase or register for your baby shower.** Consider a few popular baby gadgets:

❑ Sophie La Girafe® Teething Toy

❑ Bumbo® Multi-Seat

❑ Keekaroo® Peanut Changer in Grey (baby changing space)

❑ Stokke® MyCarrier™ 3-in-1 Front and Back Carrier in Black

❑ Baby K'tan® Wrap or Small Baby Carrier

❑ Ergobaby™ Carrier Front Facing

❑ UPPAbaby® Cruz® Stroller in Jake

❑ Boon® Naked 2-Position Bathtub (two types)

❑ Little Toader™ AppeTEETHERS™ Broccoli Bites™ in Green

❑ WubbaNub™ Brand The Original Pacifier or Plush Animal Combo

❑ Ju-Ju-Be™ B.F.F. Diaper Bag in the Duchess

❑ DockATot™

❑ Boppy® Pillow

❑ Medela Pump in Style® Advanced On-the-go Tote and Double Electric Breast Pump

❑ Twin Z Pillow® for feeding (for twins)

Hair Plan

You may want to create a plan for your hair if you're hoping to look like Kate Middleton after giving birth. Rare is the mother who wants to go take a shower after giving birth and before photo opportunities. Planning ahead can minimize this dilemma.

You can opt for a no-fuss hairstyle ahead of time that you can easily put together before heading to the hospital, such as a classic hair bun. It's also easy to bring supplies with you, such as a flat iron, blow dryer, dry shampoo, and a makeup bag for last-minute touch-ups. If you're one of those people who loves to share your pictures on social media, you may want to plan for your best friend or long-time hairdresser to be available for an on-call blowout at the hospital.

Remember filters are your friends, and one of the best is the black and white option. It can do wonders to hide any red blotchy patches on your face when you want those immediate after birth photos. These photographs will likely be around for decades, so there's nothing wrong with wanting to look your best. Of course, if you're planning a C-section you will have a little bit of a jump on good hair, but it's well worth considering your options either way.

"Before my baby shower, I bought myself a diaper bag with removable backpack straps for traveling. It's black and white—it's an amazing bag. So many pockets inside, super light, comes with a memory foam changing pad, and purse compartments in front, so I don't have to carry a purse too. It's waterproof and stain resistant. I love it!"

Mira, age 41

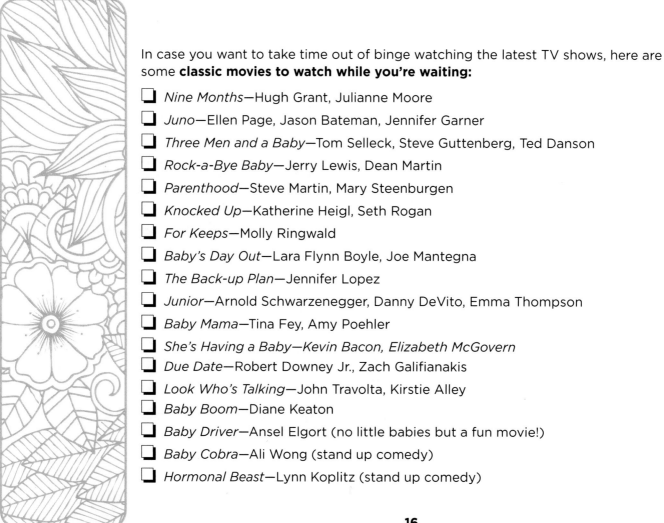

In case you want to take time out of binge watching the latest TV shows, here are some **classic movies to watch while you're waiting:**

- ❏ *Nine Months*—Hugh Grant, Julianne Moore
- ❏ *Juno*—Ellen Page, Jason Bateman, Jennifer Garner
- ❏ *Three Men and a Baby*—Tom Selleck, Steve Guttenberg, Ted Danson
- ❏ *Rock-a-Bye Baby*—Jerry Lewis, Dean Martin
- ❏ *Parenthood*—Steve Martin, Mary Steenburgen
- ❏ *Knocked Up*—Katherine Heigl, Seth Rogan
- ❏ *For Keeps*—Molly Ringwald
- ❏ *Baby's Day Out*—Lara Flynn Boyle, Joe Mantegna
- ❏ *The Back-up Plan*—Jennifer Lopez
- ❏ *Junior*—Arnold Schwarzenegger, Danny DeVito, Emma Thompson
- ❏ *Baby Mama*—Tina Fey, Amy Poehler
- ❏ *She's Having a Baby*—Kevin Bacon, Elizabeth McGovern
- ❏ *Due Date*—Robert Downey Jr., Zach Galifianakis
- ❏ *Look Who's Talking*—John Travolta, Kirstie Alley
- ❏ *Baby Boom*—Diane Keaton
- ❏ *Baby Driver*—Ansel Elgort (no little babies but a fun movie!)
- ❏ *Baby Cobra*—Ali Wong (stand up comedy)
- ❏ *Hormonal Beast*—Lynn Koplitz (stand up comedy)

My Child's Name

I have no name:
I am but two days old—
What shall I call thee?
I happy am.
Joy is my name,—
Sweet joy befall thee!
William Blake, "Infant Joy" (partial poem)

The names I am thinking about for my child and my reasons...

My child's name is officially...

It was an easy/difficult (circle) decision because...

My mood today is (draw it)...

Tip: Whether it's a boy or a girl, siblings tend to be a little heavier than the first baby. The average baby weighs 7.5 pounds and is 20 inches long. This baby is my _____ (first, second, third) and weighs _____.

Joke: *Why didn't the baby want to be born naturally?*
He didn't want to be a pain.

Birth Plan

_____

_____

_____

_____

_____

_____

_____

_____

_____

> *"My friends and I would talk about our birth plans: I mean we had it down to exactly how it's going to go and I mean there was no birth plan. I know our stories are different, but they definitely did not go the way we were talking about them when we were pregnant at prenatal yoga."*
>
> **Kara,** age 27

First-Time Mom to a Premature Baby

Sherri is a 33-year-old interior designer, and her husband is a 31-year-old technology consultant. They recently bought a house and moved to Portland, Oregon from San Francisco, California to start their family. She has a sister and a brother. Her sister has a toddler who was born at nine pounds. Sherri thought her baby would be similar. As a healthy mother in a non-risk age group, Sherri was excited to welcome her newborn into the world. Life has a way of changing the best-laid plans and to her surprise, her baby came earlier than anyone had anticipated. Sherri's baby, Hazel, was born at 32 weeks and five days. She weighed four pounds and four ounces.

"My sister was in town visiting and my husband's mom was in town. They had an overlapping visit because they wanted to see us before we had her, and then for no reason, my water broke right before dinner. There's no reason that they know of why this happened.

I went to the hospital and then approximately 13 hours later she was born. I had a natural birth (with an epidural). We were pretty nervous, but it was more nerve-wracking when she had to have a feeding tube for three weeks and a breathing machine called a CPAP for continuous positive airway pressure.

I only spent the first night in the hospital. After that, we slept at home, but spent 12 to 16 hours a day there. We were crying a lot; we were so overwhelmed. It was too stressful to stay at the hospital while we watched her grow stronger.

Once they confirmed my water broke they had tried to stop the contractions. The hospital we planned for could only deliver babies born 35 weeks on, and my baby was 32 weeks so my planned doctor was not able to deliver."

One out of 10 babies in the United States are born premature, which is considered 37 weeks or sooner, according to the March of Dimes and Centers for Disease and Prevention.

"They tried to give me magnesium, so basically I was super high—smiling—but it was terrible due to the nausea. I was dilated two centimeters. It was almost 13 hours from when my water broke until I delivered versus my mother's pregnancy with my brother which was 36 hours.

I just put all my trust into the nurses and doctors. They gave us a crash course in parenting. We changed her diaper every day and we fed her. I love breastfeeding.

She's six weeks in a few days. She's pretty normal. She can do things like go to a public area outdoors with space. She's so tiny we have to put extra cushioning in her car seat to make sure she has enough support. We disinfected our car: it's so clean. Even though the doctor gave us clearance to take her out, we're still keeping her at home most of the time.

We go once a week to the pediatrician and lactation consultant to weigh her. We still give her a bottle every day. The size of the nipple on the bottle is preemie size. It's been a challenge. She gets so hungry and then she'll spit up more than usual because she can't handle too much at one time.

She's five pounds and five ounces now. She's so easy to carry. In the house, we just carry her in our arms. In the hospital, we had a lactation consultant come by every three days because I was very adamant to breastfeed. They offered me a nipple guard but she didn't need it at all. She was one of the few breastfed babies in the premature baby wing at the hospital.

Her original due date is two weeks away. By that time, we probably won't have to get her weighed anymore, and then we can wait for her two-month checkup."

Premature Baby Facts

In the United States, about one in 10 babies are born prematurely. March of Dimes, a foundation dedicated to saving babies by preventing birth defects, premature births, and infant mortality, says the rate of premature births in the United States is 9.8%.

In Canada, the premature birth rate is slightly less. In 2013, there were 380,323 recorded births in Canada, and of those 29,715, or about 7.8%, were premature births. Between 2000 and 2013, the premature birth rate never dipped lower than 7.3% or higher than 8% (Statistics Canada).

Premature babies who are born before 22 weeks have a low chance of surviving, but there's still hope!

In 2017, NBA star J.R. Smith had a baby girl named Dakota who was born 21 weeks early weighing just one pound. She has since survived and is at home with her family.

Two children entered the *Guinness Book of World Records* for surviving birth at 21 weeks. James Elgin Gill was born 120 days premature to parents Brenda and James Gill in Ottawa, Ontario on May 20, 1987. Baby Frieda was born 21 weeks and five days early in Germany on November 7, 2010. She was the surviving baby of twins, measuring only 11 inches and weighing one pound.

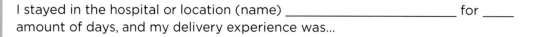

"Everybody was bustling about in a very annoying way, plumping pillows, chattering away about centimeters of dilation, and how strong the baby's heartbeat sounded. Nobody seemed to have any interest in my heartbeat, and nobody, but nobody, was getting the picture here. I was not having a good time."

Adair Lara,
Welcome to Earth, Mom

Delivery

"One pain like this should be enough to save the world forever." Toi Derricotte, *Natural Birth*

I would describe my delivery as...

When I delivered my baby it was different than I thought because...

I stayed in the hospital or location (name) _____ for ____ amount of days, and my delivery experience was...

If I knew how it was going to go, I would have chosen to...

FYI:
If you chose a natural birth or had complications, you may have had a challenging labor, but Carmelina Fedele of Aversa, Italy might disagree. In 1955, Fedele gave birth to the heaviest healthy baby ever, meaning no extenuating circumstances caused this heavy weight (*Guinness World Records*).

Joke:
Of course, I didn't watch Game of Thrones *while giving birth that would be ridiculous. I scheduled my C-section for Monday.*

The other parent...

_____

_____

_____

_____

_____

The Beginning—Date

My mother groan'd! my father wept
Into the dangerous world I leapt:
Helpless, naked, piping loud;
Like a fiend hid in a cloud.

Struggling in my father's hands
Striving against my swaddling bands:
Bound and weary I thought best
To sulk upon my mother's breast.

> William Blake, "Infant Sorrow" (partial poem)

When I saw my baby for the first time I thought...

During my first days as a mom, I...

Who is crying more, you or your baby? ;)

Taking my child in the car for the first time was...

Looking back at the birth/adoption (circle) I think it went....

I fed my baby formula/breast milk (circle) _____ minutes/hours (circle) after giving birth/adopting. Did you use a lactation consultant? If so, what's that person's name and how did it go?

Tip: If you choose to breastfeed, the best time to start is within the first hour(s) after the baby is born, according to the American Academy of Pediatrics and the World Health Organization.

What I want to remember...

Month One

Week One—Date

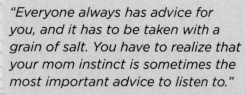

"Everyone always has advice for you, and it has to be taken with a grain of salt. You have to realize that your mom instinct is sometimes the most important advice to listen to."

Janelle, age 23

The people in the delivery room were...

I chose them to be there because...

Write the checklist you go through when your baby cries to solve the problem...

What have you learned so far?

I am feeding my baby by...

Baby Massage:

"My baby loves massages so much his first words were Burke Williams." ;) Research shows that giving your baby body massages at an early stage after childbirth can be helpful for ameliorating **jaundice.** Studies concluded that 15 minutes of baby body rubs twice a week for six weeks resulted in babies sleeping more, fussing less and having reduced stress thanks to the endorphins released by the brain during massages *(Italian Journal of Pediatrics).*

Mommy Massage:

Mom: "Hey wait, a second, I could use a massage, too!" Don't despair! The company Brookstone® might be able to help you. I use my portable plug-in Brookstone® neck and shoulder massager with a heat function on a daily basis!

Feeding Baby

"My baby was bottle fed from the start. If you give him beer on tap he rejects it every time." ;)

One of the rites of passage of becoming a mother is making decisions for your child. And one of the first decisions you will find yourself making is how you choose to feed your child.

Something that sounds so simple can easily turn into a much bigger deal than you ever imagined. You may need to make choices you had never envisioned, and the choices you planned may change. Making an informed decision is the mature thing to do; however, it is important to remember that ultimately what works best for you and your family is very likely the right one.

❏ The World Health Organization (WHO) and the American Academy of Pediatrics (AAP) recommend breastfeeding exclusively for the first six months. Then,

"My baby had jaundice because it took quite a few days for my milk to come in. Looking back, I wish I had given him a formula bottle, in addition to trying to attach the formula to a feeding tube near my chest, because it would have taken off a huge amount of stress. It's a very primal feeling to worry about whether your baby is getting enough sustenance. Soon my milk came in and I was able to feed him the whole 15 months."

Linda, age 46

begin to add complementary foods and continue for another six months (AAP) or two years (WHO).

- ☐ On average, an American mom tends to wean her child in six months.
- ☐ The World Health Organization says that less than 40% of children are breastfed exclusively.
- ☐ If you are breastfeeding, you may be living in an area where breastfeeding is common. Studies show that regardless of race, age, income or marital status, women tend to do whatever their peers are doing.

Tip: There's a rumor floating around that the hops in low-alcohol or stout beer can help breast milk production. It turns out the hops have no effect! It's the beer powder, barley extract, and malt extract that contribute to the increase in prolactin. Prolactin is the hormone responsible for initiating lactation in women. It may be that a non-alcoholic beer a day for Mom can contribute to a calm and happy baby!

Molly, Mother of Two—Breastfeeding baby

Molly is a married mother of two in her early 40s, who lives in Venice, California. She teaches Pilates, and her husband is a writer. She had her first baby at age 39 and another at 41.

> "With my first baby it's now become like old hat. At first I was terrified of breastfeeding and I had a lot of trouble doing it. I got a lactation consultant to help.

My lactation consultant helped me come up with positions that I hadn't tried and I was willing to do whatever it took to get there. I really wanted to give up in the first six weeks.

The lactation consultant's presence was very comforting; part of it was giving her my burden, and she didn't make me feel bad that I couldn't do it. She came only twice. Then, I was able to do it.

With my second baby, it's been pretty easy except she was tongue-tied, the tip of her tongue was attached. She had a procedure when she was one day old and I've heard that can cause a lot of breastfeeding problems."

Beth, First-Time Mother—When breastfeeding doesn't go as planned...

Beth is a first-time mom, age 36, who lives in Santa Clarita, California. She's a television producer and her husband is studying to be a psychologist. Her story is about the notion of breastfeeding revisited.

Beth and her husband were newlyweds when they decided to have a baby. Beth considered herself an older mom and she read up on everything about being pregnant.

"I ended up having a really beautiful, very painful natural birth so I was like, 'Yay! I did it.' And then all of a sudden there was the breastfeeding thing and I did not do anything to prepare for that.

I barely talked about breastfeeding in my childbirth education class. I had this dream scenario and the only thing I would say is that I really hope I can breastfeed for a year and possibly work during the day and that's my goal. I didn't really understand the logistics involved.

After my baby was born, he got really bad jaundice right away, and he was diagnosed with acid reflux after his first week...so pretty much the worst case scenario for me to breastfeed. Pretty much everything he did made it hard for him to suck.

I was in the hospital for two days. Everybody had different suggestions and I listened to ALL of them. He latched great and it was hella painful but I was like we are gonna do this—we're totally gonna do this— but a week later my supply wasn't that big. I started taking all these supplements. I went to a lactation consultant. I went to a support group."

Lactation consultant

"I ended up having to drive from Santa Clarita to Sherman Oaks to see this lady. She would weigh the baby and then ask me to feed the baby and then tell me how much milk I was producing. The cost was $150 for an hour session.

She talked to me about different positions, and how he's getting food, and how to keep him awake because his jaundice was making him really sleepy. My diagnosis was literally to feed him on my left breast for 10 minutes and then my right breast for 10 minutes and then pump for 10 minutes, while my husband gives him formula."

Trying everything

"The fact that we were giving him formula broke my heart instantly. And I was fighting it. I'm like, 'I'm going to get my supply up, it's going to happen!' So I'm taking all of the supplements and spending a shit ton of money ordering all these things online, drinking the teas, getting the pump that fits correctly, and it was all-consuming.

And there he is, every three hours needing to eat, and because he was such a slow eater—because his stomach was hurting him so badly—I felt like it was Groundhog Day.

I kept telling my husband, 'It's fucking Groundhog Day!' Excuse my language—(chuckles). It is the exact same thing every day. When is this going to end? And nothing seemed to work.

Every little ounce of milk I would produce he would spit up, but he would keep down the formula.

We ended up putting him on a specific diet for acid reflux and nine times out of 10 he would keep the whole thing down. So it was like what's best for my baby? What's best for me? I'm losing my sanity trying to maintain this. At about four weeks I knew I wasn't going to do it for that much longer.

I was kind of like, 'Okay, this has got to stop.'"

Creating time limits

"So I decided to make it to six weeks. I will pump and mix the breast milk with formula, or we'll just give it to him intermittently in a bottle and hope for the best.

And I ended up freezing a few rounds of pumped milk just in case someday he did not have acid reflux.

At six weeks, I decided I was done and we switched completely to formula.

My husband and I kept talking about it because his idea was, you know, whatever makes you happy. I hate seeing you so stressed. I totally support you if you want to go full formula. I know it's your decision, but I support you."

Revising expectations

"I had this fantasy about how our birth would go and it went better than planned, so I thought of course breastfeeding will be easy, but I had no idea how hard it was. And it really came with a lot of shame and guilt because there are all these people that shame you for not breastfeeding, and then there are all these people that shame you for breastfeeding in public. You can't win."

Fact: The world record for the most women breastfeeding simultaneously was 3,541, set in Manila, Philippines, on May 4, 2006 (*Guinness World Records*).

Week Two—Date

"I used to be a reasonably careless person before I had children; now I am morbidly obsessed by seat-belts and constantly afraid that low-flying aircraft will drop on my children's school."

Margaret Drabble, *Children—A Brief History of My Addiction*

The most memorable thing that happened this week was...

When I was pregnant I didn't expect...

My baby surprises me because he/she...

I'm not getting enough sleep because...

I'm going to try_____so I can sleep more.

I find I'm fearful about...

Week Three—Date

"My baby is sleeping through the night. Unfortunately, he's on London time." ;)

My plan for where my child will sleep is...

The toughest part of my week was when...

When I take the baby out in public...

The baby looks like...

I feel grateful for...

"I never expected the fear you feel as a parent. It happened right away. I've never been scared of people or places so the fear about not being able to provide, not be there to see her grow up, the fear was unimaginable to me, it never occurred to me."

Susanna, *age 42*

Revising Fairy Tales to Raise an Empowered Daughter: When you have a baby, you receive books to read to them. As you start to look at children's books for your baby's room, it's fun to think about what you can teach your little ones. Diane Keaton's character J.C. Wiatt in the movie, *Baby Boom,* recites a bedtime story to her baby girl.

"And then the prince kissed Sleeping Beauty *and she woke up and looked into the prince's eyes and you know what she said? She said thank you for waking me prince, because you know what I did, I overslept. And I have medical school today and you know I'm going to be a very important doctor one day, like all women can be. And then you know what they did? They made a date to meet each other after her graduation."*

Tip: Controversial book by Hamer and Copeland, *Living With Our Genes,* gives examples of research demonstrating which traits children inherit from their mothers and which traits they inherit from their fathers. Sorry Mom, research says you're to blame if your child snores (Doubleday).

Week Four—Date

"He slept for four hours in a row. It feels like a miracle."
                    Anne Lamott, *Operating Instructions*
"Every experience is a success."
                    Louise L. Hay, *You Can Heal Your Life*

I never expected...

I have made a personal resolution to...

When I'm holding my baby I feel...

Without the _____ (baby equipment) I don't know what I would do.

I'm starting to feel back to my normal self because...
(Weight, memory loss, social contact, etc.)

Fact:
In 2017, the most common age of American women having children was 30 to 34, narrowly surpassing the leading age group from 2016, which was 25 to 29 (Centers for Disease Control and Prevention). As of 2011, the average age of a first-time mother in the United States was 25.6, while in Canada it was 28.1 (Central Intelligence Agency). The year 2010 marked the first time that the number of Canadian women giving birth between ages 35 and 39 was higher than their counterparts aged 20 to 24 (Statistics Canada). How old are you? ____.

Checklist

☐ Action plan for the best use of your time while the baby is sleeping:

☐ How are you going to be able to do your errands? What systems can you put in place?

☐ **Mom Fitness Tip for Month One:** *"I would recommend being very gentle with the exercising right away. I remember I took a yoga class and felt totally wrecked. I underestimated the toll giving birth had taken on my body. Lay low and let your body heal—even a little bit the first month. At least physiologically that was my experience and having been in the hospital as a nursing student seeing so many women having babies for the first time."* Linda, age 39

- ❏ When you are ready—how are you going to exercise? What if your babysitter doesn't show up? Some options include the following: a digital exercise format; stream a video; put baby in a stroller (jogging strollers often need an insert to fit a smaller size baby); strap the baby to you and hike; swimming pools and gyms have babysitting services; having a small set of weights and a yoga mat at home can also help.

- ❏ What other things can you do so that you don't feel as if you are waiting?

- ❏ Learn about baby health (Sleep apnea, infant reflux, jaundice…)

- ❏ Take a nap yourself.

- ❏ **Laundry** *What do you call a mom in a laundry room? Unhappy. ;)*
  If you can afford laundry drop off, find the nearest and cleanest place. Having a newborn is the time to indulge. There are also laundry diaper services. Plan a system to minimize having an overwhelming amount of laundry to do. If you go to a laundromat, it is very helpful to find one with double, triple, or even up to six or 12 load machines. Forget about one load at a time.

- ❏ **Realize that proximity rules.** It may be time to change habits that have you driving farther than you need to go. Create a list of the nearest places for car washes, restaurants (delivery options), gyms, etc. so that you can reserve what free time you have for other things.

Checklist

Check off what your baby has and describe your experience:

❏ Jaundice

❏ Sleep apnea

❏ Infant/acid reflux

❏ Sleeping problems

❏ Colic

❏ Breastfeeding problems

❏ _____ and because of this _____.

Month in Review

You did it! You're off to the races; you've made it through the emotions of the **first month.** It's a big transition. I remember when I had my baby we just felt like we were "waiting" all the time. I'm not sure what for exactly, but mostly for someone to come and pick him up and we'd go back to our regular routine. Our life was definitely not the same. We had our baby in a time period when people still had home phones and were just beginning to have cell phones. It was not typical for people to be filming. Yet, there we were often videotaping our baby at breakfast at a local restaurant, which was assuredly not something we did before. We also sat around a lot more with a lot of staring at the baby. We watched more television shows. We had a winter baby near the holidays and there was lots of seeing friends and family. Look at your month and reflect on all you've learned and write down anything you want to remember.

❑ **Recap:** How did the pictures from your baby's birth turn out? Did you end up using a lactation consultant? Do you feel like you've watched any of your baby's milestones? What are your goals for next month? Did you change some of your habits for errands or laundry? Did you have to change your expectations in any way? What did you learn?

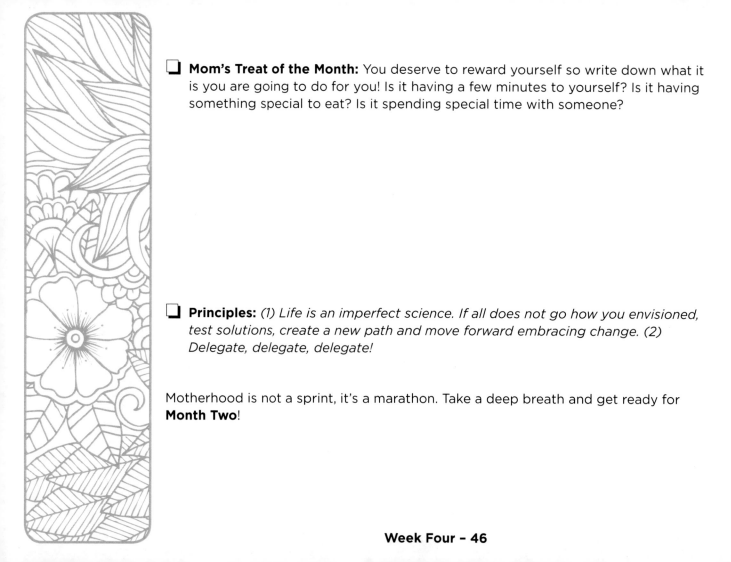

❏ **Mom's Treat of the Month:** You deserve to reward yourself so write down what it is you are going to do for you! Is it having a few minutes to yourself? Is it having something special to eat? Is it spending special time with someone?

❏ **Principles:** *(1) Life is an imperfect science. If all does not go how you envisioned, test solutions, create a new path and move forward embracing change. (2) Delegate, delegate, delegate!*

Motherhood is not a sprint, it's a marathon. Take a deep breath and get ready for **Month Two**!

CHAPTER TWO

Month Two

Week Five—Date

"Now the thing about having a baby—and I can't be the first person to have noticed this—is that thereafter you have it."

Jean Kerr, *Please Don't Eat The Daisies*

The most memorable thing that happened this week was...

My mood this week was...

When I plan my future, I want to...

My child's christening/baptism/coming to earth party is...

Where is your baby sleeping these days?

Joke: *Living in a tiny apartment with a loud crying baby, I'm always so nervous my neighbor is going to leave a mean note under my door. Luckily, he's a millennial so he never has a pen.*

Tip: **Teapots and Coffee Pots:** This suggestion is for young new moms who may not have lived in their own home for very long: consider investing in a timed coffee pot or plug-in teapot for the morning. You can prepare your coffee the night before when you're not exhausted. If you prefer tea in the morning, or if you enjoy hot water and lemon juice, the plug-in teapot heats up much faster than boiling water traditionally, and there is no chance of leaving it on the top of the stove and forgetting about it. Plug-in teapots cost as little as $20 new.

Week Six—Date

"Romance fails us—and so do friendships—but the relationship—Mother and Child—remains indelible and indestructible—the strongest bond upon this earth."

Theordore Reik, *Mothers*

The thing I like best about myself as a mother is...

What I miss from my pre-child days is...

Finding time to exercise is...

Our sleeping arrangement for our baby at this point is...

Today I'm grateful for...

Joke: *Why did the mom worry her baby would become a pyromaniac? Because he was already melting her heart.*

Tip: **Birth Control:** According to the World Health Organization, exclusive breastfeeding in the first six months is a 98% effective method of birth control.

Fact: The greatest officially recorded number of children born to a human mother is 69 and it happened in the 1700s. A peasant in Russia gave birth to 16 pairs of twins, seven sets of triplets and four sets of quadruplets. Only two of the children failed to survive their infancy (*Guinness World Records*).

Week Seven—Date

"All the parents I know are doing impossible tasks every moment."

Helen Hunt, in *Ladies' Home Journal*

My baby's favorite song is...

The most comical baby-related incident was when...

I'm looking forward to...

I keep forgetting to...
(Brush teeth, wash hair, send thank you cards, open my eyes fully etc.)

If I had to pick a famous person that looks likes my child I would say...

My napping philosophy is...

Baby Bones: Grown-ups have exactly 206 bones, but experts disagree about exactly how many bones babies have—most say somewhere between 270 and the low 300s. The most popular view is that **babies' skeletons have around 300 distinct parts,** many of which are made of cartilage, and which eventually fuse to create the adult skeleton (*Mammal Anatomy, BBC Science*).

Moms With Some Good News

"I'm a super planner. I mean my baby came three weeks early, and before that I was sitting around tapping my fingers. But I have been pleasantly surprised that most of the things people scared me about have not come true!"

Lindsey, an organized married mother of one

"I thought I would hate changing diapers etc. and it would be terrible but it's not so bad."

Susanna, a mother who chose a donor and to do it on her own

"I can't believe that I'm able to do this. I've watched my sisters and friends and it just seems so hard and I have been like I don't know if I can do that. Then, you have a baby and you just do it. I mean, it's so amazing, but you just do it. You wake up and change diapers and you just kind of do it and it's so amazing."

Molly, one of five siblings including three sisters with children

"As an older mom, I was surprised at how much energy I felt and how strong I was. I wanted to be truly present and not miss any of it, so this was an unexpected happy surprise."

Linda, a mom with a retired hubby

Week Eight—Date

"The most sensitive, most delicate of instruments—the mind of a little child!"
Henry Handel Richardson, *Ultima Thule*

Has your baby lifted his/her head up today? Have you?

The first thing my baby likes to do when he/she wakes up is...

My baby's sleeping pattern is...

How are you doing with immunizing your baby?

Have you tried using a musical mobile? Does your baby like it?

What's your baby's favorite song?

Music Tips

❀ The "Smile Song" from the television show, *My Little Pony: Friendship is Magic*, was written and composed by my brother, Daniel Ingram. If you and your baby are needing a pick-me-up, it's sure to be a mood changer. It's available on YouTube.

❀ **According to the Journal of the Acoustical Society of America, a two-month-old infant can remember a short melody and differentiate it from a similar melody.**

Joke: *Does your baby listen to lullabies? No, he prefers Kid Rock.*

Checklist

☐ Throw previous expectations of motherhood out of the door.

☐ Be grateful for sleep.

☐ **Don't criticize yourself for not losing weight.** Make a decision to not judge yourself for a year—don't give up, but give yourself a break.

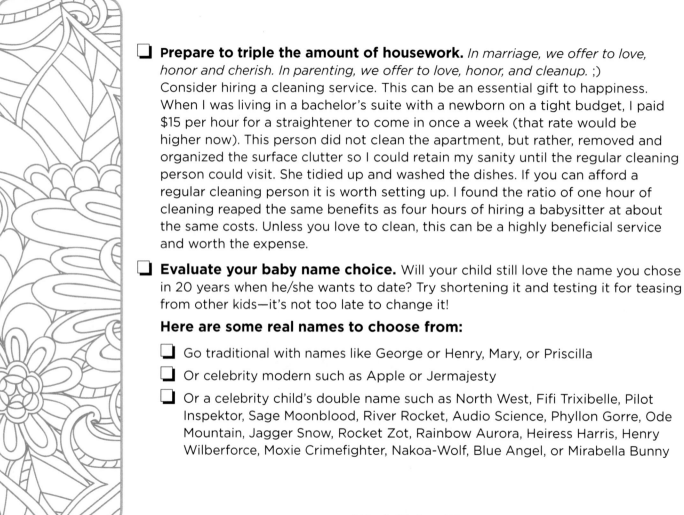

❑ **Prepare to triple the amount of housework.** *In marriage, we offer to love, honor and cherish. In parenting, we offer to love, honor, and cleanup.* ;) Consider hiring a cleaning service. This can be an essential gift to happiness. When I was living in a bachelor's suite with a newborn on a tight budget, I paid $15 per hour for a straightener to come in once a week (that rate would be higher now). This person did not clean the apartment, but rather, removed and organized the surface clutter so I could retain my sanity until the regular cleaning person could visit. She tidied up and washed the dishes. If you can afford a regular cleaning person it is worth setting up. I found the ratio of one hour of cleaning reaped the same benefits as four hours of hiring a babysitter at about the same costs. Unless you love to clean, this can be a highly beneficial service and worth the expense.

❑ **Evaluate your baby name choice.** Will your child still love the name you chose in 20 years when he/she wants to date? Try shortening it and testing it for teasing from other kids—it's not too late to change it!

Here are some real names to choose from:

❑ Go traditional with names like George or Henry, Mary, or Priscilla

❑ Or celebrity modern such as Apple or Jermajesty

❑ Or a celebrity child's double name such as North West, Fifi Trixibelle, Pilot Inspektor, Sage Moonblood, River Rocket, Audio Science, Phyllon Gorre, Ode Mountain, Jagger Snow, Rocket Zot, Rainbow Aurora, Heiress Harris, Henry Wilberforce, Moxie Crimefighter, Nakoa-Wolf, Blue Angel, or Mirabella Bunny

- ❏ There's the triple or quadruple name option such as Zuma Nesta Rock or Diva Thin Muffin Pigeen
- ❏ Another option is the first name last name combo, such as Jute Box, Tu Morrow, Sandy Beach, or my pal Greg's brainchild, also a real name, Justin Case
- ❏ Or there is always the accidental first name, last name combo. When you love the name Rose, but you end up marrying a man with the last name Bush

❏ Tackle the breast pump situation. Decide if it is for you.

Stella Establishes a Winning Schedule

Stella, is a working first-time mother with twins who lives in Pacific Palisades, California, with her husband. She shares her breast pumping and feeding schedule.

"I was already working the second week after my delivery. But that's because my kids were healthy and I was healthy. I didn't have a C-section. I had a natural birth."

Stella had a schedule where she fed her twins every two hours whether she breastfed or used bottles providing her own milk that had been stored.

"Between midnight and four am they would not wake up (whether they trained me or I trained them) but at four am, six am, eight am, I

fed them. I had an alarm [for myself at two am] and that would be my surplus extra. I made mistakes that I didn't store it properly etc., but for the most part, I would gather up that extra feeding for work times.

Your kids leave an internal note to make as much as you need so I stuck with it. If you start supplementing, then you might not make enough but I kept going every two hours on the dot."

Stella—Twins Breastfeeding Tips:

"I didn't use any pillows. They would each straddle my side and I would be in an upright position so they didn't choke, and I heard it helps avoid ear infections. I would bounce on the bouncy ball at the same time. Once in a while, we would be in bed and if one passed out I would pass that child to my husband, but mostly I fed them upright and facing me." Stella, age 34, a married mother of twins

Kati—Twins Breastfeeding Tips:

"I'm still using the Twin Z Pillow®. It's kind of like a Boppy Pillow® except it's for twins. It's one big pillow with two little holes. It's an amazing thing for twins." Kati, age 37, a married mother of twins plus one

Month in Review

Two months into your new life already! For me, it was the six-week mark that was a big one. It was at that point, I gathered up my little muscular bundle of joy (I know, weird but he had little muscular baby legs and I actually recognized his real-life foot from him kicking me in the abdomen while I was pregnant! Ouch!) and we boarded an airplane from the West Coast to the East Coast to resume my second semester of school at a journalism program. It was very scary to think of taking my young baby boy on an airplane. Sometimes you just have to take each "baby" step and just do the next stage of your plan, cross your fingers and hope for the best. We arrived in one piece, and my friends picked us up at the airport. I was in a small university program of forty students and all of our classes were in one building. It was strange to walk up those steps with a baby in tow, not knowing how people would react. They had seen me pregnant throughout the first semester but not met my son. But again, one day at a time. You just move forward with your goals.

❏ **Recap:** How is your body doing? Have you settled into any routines? Have you figured out what baby equipment you need and like? Have you had any thoughts about your baby's christening or the religious ceremony associated with your family? Have you figured out how your baby is going to meet everyone?

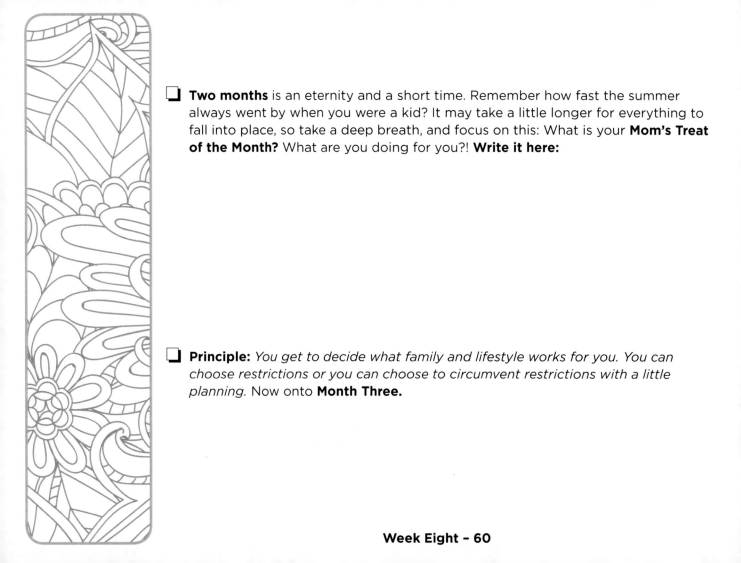

❏ **Two months** is an eternity and a short time. Remember how fast the summer always went by when you were a kid? It may take a little longer for everything to fall into place, so take a deep breath, and focus on this: What is your **Mom's Treat of the Month?** What are you doing for you?! **Write it here:**

❏ **Principle:** *You get to decide what family and lifestyle works for you. You can choose restrictions or you can choose to circumvent restrictions with a little planning.* Now onto **Month Three.**

CHAPTER THREE

Month Three

Week Nine—Date

"My children were a constant joy to me, except on days when they weren't."

Evelyn Fairbanks, *The Days of Rondo*

Today I'm grateful for...

What is a physical feature you love on your baby? (Big eyelashes, cute feet, etc.)...

I'm introducing the new baby to...

My philosophy on Tylenol®, Dimetapp®, homeopathic teething pills, etc. is...

Family members I can rely on are...

What are your plans to visit relatives who don't live nearby but would like to see the baby?

Book Recommendation

The Essential Grandparent by Lillian Carson. Relatives can be a valuable resource when raising a child. Sometimes all it takes is asking the question.

Mother of Twins

"Both my parents came and stayed with us for the first six weeks so that kept me sane. If they didn't come I don't know what I would have done. One person is not enough for twins, you need to have at least two people there at all times, especially if you have a third child like we do."

Kati, first-time mother of twins and an older sibling

Week Ten—Date

"When I first accidentally banged my child's head into something, I was so ashamed. It was a dirty little secret I kept from dad. Now I just go, 'Oh well, comfort him and move on."

Nicky, working mother of two

I should win an award for coordination because...

My baby likes to...

I love my partner, but...

I learned about the four-month sleep progression of babies because...

I learned about attachment parenting and I agree/disagree (circle) because...

Finding Sleep

"Sleep deprivation—isn't that a torture method?—It's a real thing."

Lindsey, age 30, Arizona married mom

"It wasn't that the baby didn't sleep. I couldn't sleep! A struggle I had in the beginning was a bit of insomnia when we first brought her home. Not being able to sleep, period. You get paranoid that the baby is not okay, so it's really hard to fall asleep, even though you're exhausted."

Sarah, working single mother

Alison—How a Sleep Consultation Saved Me From Sleep Deprivation

Alison is the mother of a four-year-old daughter and 15-month-old boy. She is a 38-year-old, long-time married mother and journalist who lives in Calgary, Alberta. She found herself with a seemingly insurmountable sleeping issue after her second child was born.

"We just seemed to get farther down into our hole and we just didn't know what to do. It seemed hopeless. Everything we tried just resulted in more screaming."

Until she hired a sleep consultant...

Sleep consultant

"She talked to me. I filled out a questionnaire. I talked to her for an hour. Then she came up with a plan that involved removing one of his naps and changing his schedule around a little bit. We removed any props that could be associated with sleep or that involved nursing.

Now six weeks out, I read him a couple of stories, sing him a little song, walk away and 12 hours later he wakes up."

Checklist

❏ **Prioritize your errands:** By now hopefully, you are no longer doing one errand at a time, instead you are finding ways to prioritize the important ones, and forgetting the frivolous ones. Good job! Time management is a priority for most moms.

❏ **Take turns if you can:** If you are part of a couple, you might want to create a deck of cards. Have a third of them say, "Your Turn," and a third of them say, "Pass," and the rest can say, "You've got to be kidding, choose again in three minutes." This way, if one of you has to get up in the middle of the night to soothe the baby, the cards will determine the outcome.

- [ ] **Find moments to play:** Dress up—at least one day a week—this includes washed hair, preferably no overalls (channel your favorite singer), and wear makeup (if you wore it before).

- [ ] **Take a tip from *The Ellen DeGeneres Show* to always dance:** Try dancing around the house to music and make a mental note that confidence comes from within. If you are in search of a song try "Slip" by Stooshe.

- [ ] **Does your baby have colic?** Prepare yourself if your baby cries nonstop. It's nothing you did. **Colic** is defined by famed Dr. Morris Wessel's "Rule of three's" as crying lasting more than three hours a day, three days a week, for three weeks. The good news is that it usually stops at three months. Colic may be due to an undeveloped immune system. **Strategy:** This can be a test of true friendship. Create a decorative basket of earplugs for your guests and seek out friends who are patient, understanding, and maybe went to a few too many rock concerts, raves, or music festivals back in the day and are hard of hearing. ;)

When I went to my friend's house, her baby was strapped to her front in a baby sling while he was crying his eyes out. With a jolly laugh, she said, *"He has colic. We just have to shout."* And she puttered about the kitchen fixing me a toasted bagel and telling me about her day. She had such a positive attitude that we just talked really loudly and I remember our unique visit fondly.

Around the Clock or Baby Breaks?

Sally—Married Working Mom

Sally and her husband did not go out at night when they first had their baby. Instead, they planned several vacations to visit their families and give themselves a little break from full-time parenting duties. Since both of them have relatives that live outside of their hometown of Los Angeles, they took their baby on trips to Europe, Costa Rica and San Francisco.

"We still don't go out at night really. What we have done is taken a lot of vacations. Because we were visiting family they were also the first in line to babysit, so I can't say we didn't go out at all."

Angie—Stay-at-home Single Mom

"She's never been away from me. At this point in our relationship, I wouldn't be relaxed. It wouldn't be enjoyable for me, or her."

Sarah—Working Single Mom

"You shouldn't feel guilty because what I've realized is that having someone you are paying to give full-time dedicated attention to your kid is actually way more beneficial for them than you trying to divide your time across an entire day. Developmentally, she's benefiting a lot from having a nanny because there's someone there engaging with her one-on-one. She's not trying to do laundry, she's not trying to walk the dog. She's not trying to do all these other things simultaneously. She's just focused on my daughter. I feel less guilty now that I've gone through that. I can see that my daughter gets taken out more because the nanny is not as busy as me since that's her job."

Linda S.—Part-time Working Married Mom

"We had our baby with us most of the time, but there are all these wonderful coffee shops in Bend, Oregon where we live. We have such happy memories of sitting in those places, reading the newspaper, drinking coffee and being out."

Checklist

❑ **Baby gas:** Baby gas is often caused by an immature digestive system and your baby's inability to process milk or food items properly, or by ingesting too much air.

   ❑ Bill Murray, actor and father of six, suggested a creative solution while being interviewed on the *Jimmy Kimmel Live!* TV show. He says that the peppermint in candy canes relieves gas and colic in babies. Peppermint has been cultivated for its essential oils since the 1700s. It's the menthol ingredient in the oil that can potentially provide health benefits such as alleviating gas and an upset stomach. Of course, it might be best to choose a sugar-free alternative and save this tip for the holidays.

   ❑ Other options include baby massage, burping your baby every five minutes on average between feedings, putting warm blankets on their belly, or over-the-counter baby drops.

   ❑ You can also try avoiding certain foods, such as beans, broccoli, and cabbage.

   ❑ Additionally, it might be helpful to check with a midwife or lactation consultant to ensure you are not under- or overfeeding your baby.

❑ **Bicycle game:** Bill Murray went on to say that if your baby is not tired, try rotating his or her legs like a bicycle while the baby lies down. He says this wears them out. Worth a try!

❑ **Take a mom's swim spa break:** You may want to head to the swimming pool. After not being able to use a hot tub during your pregnancy, organize a sitter and take this time to find a soothing hot tub date with a friend or partner or even solo! It will be so nice to take a swim or relax in a spa.

Help Is Around the Corner: Services Rendered

We used a:

- ❏ Sleep Consultant
- ❏ Nanny
- ❏ Lactation Nurse
- ❏ Night Nurse
- ❏ Doula
- ❏ Babysitter
- ❏ Siblings/Grandparents/Family
- ❏ None of the above

We chose help/no help (circle) because...

Checklist

Ways to Get Involved. (Check those which you joined and describe your experience).

- ❏ Mommy and Me Classes
- ❏ Facebook Mommy Groups
- ❏ Baby Bootcamp
- ❏ Family Yoga
- ❏ Public Health Nurse Mommy Groups
- ❏ Mommy and Me Movies
- ❏ Gymboree Classes
- ❏ Baby Singing and Music Classes
- ❏ A Gym with Child Care
- ❏ Swim Classes
- ❏ Church Community Classes
- ❏ Other:

Retaining Sanity: Some Things New Moms Chose to Do to Feel Like Their Authentic Self

"I go to the gym, and make sure I dress nicely which is challenging with breastfeeding. I try not to wear comfortable frumpy clothes."

Sarah, business development

"HGTV, the Home and Garden Network, and lots of it. It's so relaxing."

Susanna, a corporate lawyer

"I always try to put makeup on when I go out. It makes me feel good. Because about three or four months into motherhood, I had been going out and noticing that I had even forgotten to brush my teeth. I was like, 'This cannot continue.' I need to do things that are going to make me feel good and I need to somewhat look after myself. I feel better in makeup. I just need to wear makeup when I go out—and brush my teeth."

Emily, food services

Retaining Sanity: Some Things New Moms Chose to Do to Feel Like Their Authentic Self Continued...

"I'm committed to making sure I shower everyday. I'm in a bunch of Mommy Facebook Groups and I would see these posts about women saying they hadn't showered in two days and I'd read blogs about not showering and I was like, 'No, this is NOT happening. I'm showering every day.' Honestly, on the weekends sometimes I wouldn't shower before I had the baby—just because it would be too much work. Because I had been working all week and I just like vegging out on the couch. I'd be marathon watching Orange is the New Black *and suddenly it's seven pm and I haven't showered and it's like, 'Oh well.' Now I'm committed to showering every single day."*

Beth, TV producer

Week Eleven—Date

"Begin, little boy, to recognize your mother with a smile."

Virgil, poet

The most memorable thing that happened this week was...

The biggest surprise I had this week was...

One thing I learned from someone else was...

I think sex is...

Aha! Breastfeeding Moment: *"My friend was breastfeeding all the time, in public, in front of friends, everywhere. I thought before I had my baby, it was something you do every three hours and then you go back to your life, and the baby's all happy, but then you realize while you're halfway through grocery shopping that she's screaming and wants the boob and you have to stop everything you're doing. It was quite an adjustment to understand this little person needs you, not every three hours or not when it's convenient for you, but when they need you. And what's the words I'm looking for? You just have to kind of get over yourself."* Emily, Kamloops, British Columbia married mom of one

Baby Still Not Sleeping? Book Tip: *Secrets of the Baby Whisperer* by Tracy Hogg and Melinda Blau (Atria Books: reprint 2006).

Joke: *Why didn't the mom want her baby sleeping in a crib? She didn't want to get him used to life behind bars.*

Week Twelve—Date

"Home alone with a wakeful newborn, I could shower so quickly that the mirror didn't fog and the backs of my knees stayed dry."

Marni Jackson, *The Mother Zone*

The most memorable thing that happened this week was...

The most trying thing I had to do this week was...

I never thought as a mother I would...

One thing I thought I would do as a mother, but I will never do is...

Do you have a favorite chair now? A rocking chair, perhaps?

Today my energy level is...

Fact: One of the reasons it's harder for women to have babies as they get older is because their eggs are as old as they are. Research indicates that if a woman wants to know how long she'll be able to have babies, finding out when her mother went into menopause is a good predictor (*Science Daily*).

Society: More men remarry than women, according to data by Pew Research Center. In 2013, 64% of previously married men had remarried compared to 52% of divorced or widowed women. The number of women remarrying is on the rise.

Joke: *Why did you have your first baby at 46—I mean isn't that a little late? Yes, but I live in LA and I forgot my real age.*

Weird Body Changes. Do You Have Any of These?

*"No one tells you that all of your **hair starts to fall out** about three to six months after having the baby. It stops but that was disturbing and shocking. It apparently happens to 60% of women. A lot of my friends have had to get bangs to cover up their receding hairline. My hair thickened up during pregnancy so I miss that. As long as you aren't missing too many nutrients you will be fine, not having certain minerals contributes."*

Sarah, age 27

Theory: Some women find that their hair grows thicker while pregnant, so what feels like hair loss three to six months after childbirth may actually be because your hair is returning to normal levels. According to American Pregnancy Association, one to five months after delivery, 40-50% of women temporarily shed excess hair or have short-term hair loss. Ask your doctor!

*"**My ears were plugged** and I'd be like, 'Sorry guys, I can't hear you because I'm pregnant.' And they'd be like, 'You're out of your mind,' and I'd say, 'That's a real thing, actually.'"*

Janelle, age 23

Theory: This may happen due to fluid retained during pregnancy (www.babycenter.com). Ask your doctor!

*"No one told me about double vision which apparently happens to some women. Your eyes **experience vision changes**. I had double vision. Apparently, hormonal changes can cause dryness in your eyes which results in the surface of your eyes being bumpier. This changes the way it refracts light. It is **temporary**...They don't really recommend changing your glasses or anything because of it. My vision actually improved, that's the other thing that's weird. The double vision happened around when the baby was three months old. It's getting a lot better now. It's going away now that I'm not breastfeeding as much, I went to the eye doctor. I was in the living room and I couldn't read the time on the TV player. I was seeing two of everything and it got so bad I couldn't read a book."*

Sarah, age 27

Theory: According to WebMD.com, some things to look out for are dry eyes (for which artificial tears can help if you're not wearing contacts), or blurred vision (impacted by a changing thickness/shape of your cornea caused by retained fluids). This usually goes away after delivery or after you stop breastfeeding. Also be aware of changes if you have diabetes. Please ask your doctor!

"I knew that breastfeeding helps you contract and go back into shape but I didn't expect that it would hurt and that I would actually feel like was having small contractions after having the baby."

Janelle, age 23

Theory: It might be called, "after pains." Ask your doctor!

"My nose was stuffed up the entire time I was pregnant and then it vanished when I had the baby."
Brynn, age 21

Theory: She might have had "pregnancy rhinitis," a condition which describes nasal congestion during pregnancy. When blood and estrogen levels shoot up it can cause swelling in the tiny blood vessels lining the inside of your nose. If you think you have this, please check with your doctor! You want to make sure your baby has all the oxygen it needs for its development.

"I kept smelling burnt coffee when I was pregnant and that went away part way through the first year of my son's life."
Jen, age 27

Theory: It might be a sinus infection or a nasal polyp. Nasal polyps are noncancerous growths that can lead to a diminished sense of smell or infection. Ask your doctor!

***My wrists were hurting so much** when I had the baby that I was having trouble lifting him and that's part of the reason I was struggling with breastfeeding. I later learned it was pregnancy induced carpal tunnel syndrome."*
Beth, age 36

Theory: I have had carpal tunnel so I know how painful it can be. I thought I might have fractured my wrist but it turned out I had carpal tunnel syndrome. Fluid retention during pregnancy can cause pressure and swelling on the relatively narrow space in the wrist bone causing this painful condition. Check with your doctor!

Checklist

For exercise (Check what you do, and how often).

☐ Walk
☐ Play
☐ Run
☐ Spin
☐ Hike
☐ Pilates
☐ Yoga
☐ Swim
☐ Gym
☐ Other:

I am able to do this because...

I exercise because...

I want to...

Month in Review

Three months already! So much to look back on. At this point, I had settled into full-time school. I realized that sleep as I knew it was a thing of the past. I discovered that I would have three days of getting absolutely nothing done while listening to endless crying, and suffering from a complete lack of sleep. Then miraculously the next three days, I would get a ton of stuff done. I would catch up on all of the schoolwork I hadn't managed, and I was able to rest. Once I realized our pattern, I had far less stress when the challenging days would come. My teachers had grown to love my baby; one teacher even offered to hold him for me while he taught our class. And I had gathered my team of student babysitters who would stay with him while I attended the classes where I was not able to bring him along. My son became a fixture in the computer room while I worked on my assignments. My favorite time of the day came around nine pm when school was over and the sky was dark. My friend would accompany me for the walk home. Right beside my apartment was a quiet little restaurant that only ever had a few regulars. We'd go in, and the layout of the restaurant allowed me to put my sleeping child and his bassinet under the table in the booth undetected. For just a short while, we'd have some social time while having a drink and a snack. Then I would go home—only a few doors down—for some much-needed rest.

❑ **Recap:** How's the sleeping going?! What strange things have happened to your body? Have any of your friendships had to adjust? Have you had to change your thinking? How is your mental state? Do you feel balanced or overwhelmed? Are you feeling optimistic or discouraged? Have you had time to exercise? Do you

feel like yourself? Have you made it to any baby classes or do you plan to go? How's your relationship moving along? Has your relationship with your relatives changed?

☐ **A quarter of the year** accomplished! Just because you did it last month, doesn't mean you don't deserve another bear hug for making it through month three! Is your baby smiling at you now? I'm sure your little one is grateful. As you get into your groove, it's that time again, don't forget it, don't neglect it, you've earned it. It's time to figure out your **Mom's Treat of the Month!** Do Not Read Further Until You Treat Yourself. If you don't want to spend an hour, fine! I'm not going to argue, but at least figure out something special for YOU and after you've treated yourself write it down here:

❏ **Principles:** *(1) It takes a village. Who can you bring into your life to simplify things? (2) Plan medical insurance and sick care. Make a plan for yourself and your baby in case one of you comes down with an unexpected illness. Who will take care of the baby? Who will take care of you?*

Get ready to open the door for **Month Four**!

What I want to remember...

CHAPTER FOUR

Month Four

Week Thirteen—Date

"Being a mother basically killed my ambition. I don't feel like someone is going to take [everything I've worked for] away. And I have this life that I love so much."

Bette Midler, performer on the *Today Show*

Relatives who are heavily involved with the baby are...

The best and worst parts of this week were...

I am feeling more back to my normal self because...

I worry about...

What's the best advice you can give to yourself?

Today, I'm grateful for...

Decorating Tip

Babies love to draw on surfaces. Moms tend to not like to clean them. There is a paint that creates a **chalkboard** on the wall. You can put it on a door or on a narrow wall, so as your baby gets older they can draw on it. You can go with a company like ECOS Interior so it's organic or low VOC. It's best not to paint with a newborn in the house! They are too sensitive, so do not have your baby nearby.

Fact: More educated women are having children by their mid-40s than in the past two decades. In 2015, only 20% of women ages 40 to 44 with a Master's degree or PhD didn't have children, compared to 30% in 1994, according to Pew Research Center.

Joke: *I believe you shouldn't separate the artist from the art. So can you tell my poorly behaved toddler I can no longer support his finger paintings?*

Mom Decides Whether to Return to Work Full-Time

When Nancy's one-year maternity leave in Alberta, Canada came to an end, she was faced with one of the biggest decisions a woman can make in her lifetime; she had to choose whether or not to return to work. As a person in a long-term economically stable marriage, Nancy didn't have to factor in the financial reasons, nor did she feel an extreme passion for her career at this point in time. But she did feel a societal pressure, plus a deep concern for the value of work and the personal efforts she'd made throughout her career. These are the kinds of decisions that can change our lives in the most important ways, and they can often result in things turning out much differently than we'd ever expect.

"I kept thinking about all of this. Am I going to go back? I probably should. I just started at a new place, but of course, in my heart I knew

that I absolutely did not want to. Yet, I felt a little pressure from society that it is so important to work.

I remember succinctly what happened. I was sitting in my daughter's room and we were coloring and we got a call from the Director in my area and he's like, 'It's time to come back to work now, and we have a job to offer you.' First of all, it was a total crumb job. It was teaching all these different subjects, and teaching a little every day and it was totally unworkable for daycare.

My mother-in-law would have taken care of my daughter but it was totally unworkable realistically and I told him, 'Okay I have a lot to think about it.' I realized there was no way I'm doing that. I had been kind of worried about it over the last month and then it was just such a huge relief, 'Oh, I don't have work.'"

Change of heart

"There was a part of me that wanted to go back to work, if it was the right job...[instead of thinking], 'Oh shoot, they gave me a shitty job and I can't go.' If they had given me the perfect opportunity, it might have been different.

Before my daughter was born, I was teaching but it was different positions. I had three contracts for about two years each. That was the other reason—I had a continuing contract that I had worked toward—so that's why it was a big decision; it wasn't just a contract position that ends but a continuing position. It was only like two years of work that

got me there, but still it felt like a big decision because people want those positions—like in the grand scheme of things—whatever—but at the time it felt like a big deal because all the young teachers are dying to get a continuing contract and I remember I had felt that way before."

Nancy thought that it would be satisfying to return to a continuing position, so she did plan to return to work after her maternity leave. Now she works part-time instead, and she is very particular about which jobs she chooses, but she doesn't regret her decision. She has been very happy as a full-time mom. Her daughter is very involved in competitive dance and her son loves to snowboard and ski.

Fact: **Stay-at-home moms are on the rise.** According to Pew Research Center, after decades of decline, there has been a recent increase in stay-at-home moms. In 2012, research demonstrated 29% of mothers stay home versus 23% in 1999. The research concluded that two-thirds of these mothers are from traditional married families.

2012	1999
29% stay-at-home moms	23% stay-at-home moms

Fact: **Women's labor force participation is on a declining trend,** according to a US Labor Bureau Statistics. In 2015, 56% of women worked, which was down from 57% in 2014. The statistics demonstrate that women's workforce participation peaked at 60% in 1999 and has been going down ever since. However, mothers encompass a larger percentage of the women who are working. In 2014, 71% of US mothers worked outside the home (Pew Research Center).

2015	2014	1999
56% of women worked	57% of women worked	60% of women worked

2014	57% of U.S. women were working	71% of the 57% women working were moms

FYI: Research demonstrates 60% of Americans say that children are better off with a parent at home. However, college-educated women are most likely to say that children are just as well off with both parents working (Pew Research Center).

Tip: **Why Moms Might Want to Keep Working.** There are more women living in poverty than men in their old age after retirement.

It's a Start: In 2018, Iceland became the first country to make it illegal to pay women less than men for doing the same job.

Week Fourteen—Date

"I want my children to have all the things I couldn't afford. Then I want to move in with them."

Phyllis Diller, comedian

I never expected...

I have made a personal resolution to...

Without the _____ (baby equipment) I don't know what I would do.

I'm starting to feel back to my normal self because...
(Weight, memory loss, social contact, etc.)

FYI: Having a child out of wedlock is not unusual in Iceland. In fact, in 2014, 70.5% of parents in Iceland had children out of wedlock *(Iceland Monitor)*. This is in stark contrast to Canada, where 33% of births were out of wedlock as of 2012 *(OECD.Stat)*. One of the reasons Iceland has so many births to unmarried parents, according to a 2003 study of demographic trends in the country, is that in Iceland there is almost no judgment on single mothers *(Eydal, Olafson)*. Iceland eliminated any legal differences between legitimate and illegitimate children in 1991.

Here are the unwed birth rates of some other notable countries:

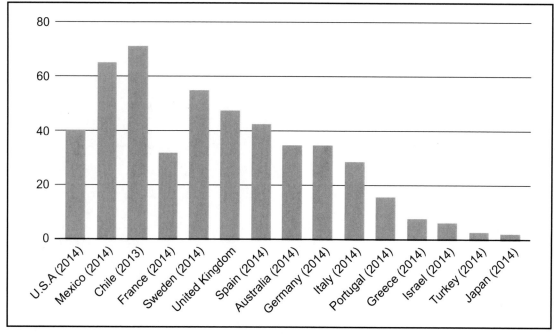

OECD.stat

Week Fifteen—Date

"The only thing which seems to me to be eternal and natural in motherhood is ambivalence."

Jane Lazarre, *The Mother Knot*

I feel proud of my child when...

When I think about working outside of the home, I feel...

The people who take care of my child are...

Fact: Working moms are three times more likely than working dads to say that being a working parent has made it a greater challenge for them to advance their careers—51% versus 16% (Pew Research Center).

Joke: *I love traveling but playing airplane with my baby is the closest I got the first year.*

Sally Stuck At Home

Sally explains how she felt housebound and what helped her overcome it. Feel free to write your own experiences about this and how you will solve it.

"The one thing for me is the feeling I was under house arrest. I couldn't go out. In the beginning I was around a lot of my friends and they were happy for me, and then the baby was born and I was in it. My husband went to work and all of a sudden I was all by myself. No one ever told me how lonely that whole process can be.

Maybe it's different across cultures and around the world because communities are set up differently, but for me I felt really alone and I felt like I couldn't go out. Sure, I can put the baby in her stroller or in a carrier but the time was very short lived because sure enough, I had to bring her back for a nap, I had to feed her, I had to change diapers. Everything had to be very convenient. I thought you just go about your day with a baby by your side, but no one told me—I didn't anticipate— how all-consuming it is."

Sally is a film makeup artist and mother of two young girls. She has been married for three years to her husband who is a creative director and they are in their mid-30s.

Tip: Go online and join a Mommy Meetup. There are often mom websites you can join that are specific to your local residential area, so you can connect with other mothers and share in baby activities and events locally.

Create fun

If you can't get out of the house, consider asking a few girlfriends to come over to join you with a Bunco party, or have a book club night. Just pick a short book!

Some of my favorite short books include:

- ❀ The Hitchhiker's Guide to the Galaxy—Douglas Adams
- ❀ The Little Prince—Antoine de Saint-Exupery
- ❀ Cakes and Ale—Somerset Maugham
- ❀ The Old Man and the Sea—Ernest Hemingway

- ❀ The House on Mango Street—Sandra Cisneros
- ❀ Me Talk Pretty One Day—David Sedaris
- ❀ An Elephant Called Butterfly—Marian Hailey Moss and Lois Meredith
- ❀ Mindset: The New Psychology of Success—Carol S. Dweck

Book Reading Tip

If you're too tired to read, take advantage of Audible or other sites that allow the book to be read to you! There are also audiobooks for babies!

Sally's Solutions—Creating Community, Taking Advantage of Social Media Sharing

When Sally's first-born was about four months old, she found it important to develop a new community of friends for herself. Sally says it was definitely about being in groups and bonding with other moms who were going on that same journey.

> *"Whether it was sleep training or teething or some of these daily issues that would come up, I had a community of women that I could talk to. They could relate to me and I could relate to them and our kids would have playdates. All of a sudden I had this community."*

She says she is still good friends with these moms. Her daughter is now two years old and four months. Sally says, *"The other aspect is like just being able, within that community,* **to share information**. *We support each other with advice or tips, 'Hey, try this app.'"* Sally says she still has times when she feels like she's under house arrest with two kids, but she's grateful for the digital age.

> *"I still feel like I am under house arrest with two kids sometimes. I don't know how it would have been before the Internet; we have so many conveniences now. So many delivery services that make getting out— the struggles of being out with a baby—so much easier."*

Week Sixteen—Date

"Why not have your first baby at sixty, when your husband is already dead and your career is over? Then you can really devote yourself to it."

Fran Lebowitz in *Redbook*

The most memorable thing that happened this week was...

I spent _____ amount of minutes/hours/days (circle) to myself this week.

My pre-pregnancy back to work plan has changed because...

What I want for myself in the next year is...

My energy level today is...

Sarah on Dating, Working, and Nanny Shares—Finding a Successful Way to Balance Single Life and Motherhood

Sarah and her partner will not stay together forever. Sarah is in her twenties. She enjoys her career, and wants to have time to develop a new relationship or find a few moments to spend time with friends. She feels she has pieced together a family dynamic that works for her newborn.

"I went back to work at six months part-time. I work in business development for a restaurant. It's really flexible. I can make my own hours.

We have part-time child care. We had an overnight nanny one night [per week] but that recently came to an end and now it's only until 1:30 am. She's a live-in nanny with another family so she would just stay one night over here. She's paid minimum wage plus food and shelter and vacation costs. We share two days a week with them, too."

Tip: According to a study by Pew Social Trends, taking care of children is more rewarding than working but more exhausting.

Another reason to keep working, even part-time: There are 20% more stay-at-home moms who lived in poverty in 2012 (34%) compared to 1970 (14%), and there was a 5% increase in how many moms said they simply could not find jobs (Pew Research Center).

Concept of a half-birthday: If your baby's birthday falls near a major holiday or a time other kids aren't around, you might consider doing a mini half-birthday celebration at the six-month point. We would get a couple of family members, maybe one or two friends, and go to the local free waterpark and kids activity place for his half-birthday in the summer. We'd open one or two presents. This offset the pressure of his birthday often falling on or near Thanksgiving.

Joke: *Sure my baby has a monitor. Me!*

Month in Review

You've finished **month four!** Ugh, you may find the real world seeping into your happy baby life. Perhaps you were just figuring out some things and the next thing you know, actual work, real-life pre-baby stresses, and people who forget you are a mother now, all present themselves. You want to scream out, "I'm busy, people!"

In my circumstance, it was getting into the routine of school and winter. Winter was a challenge. I recall walking up to my door one day only to find a snow block in my way. There was no chance a stroller was getting down that street with four feet of snow. A taxi could not get there. My baby was actually getting a little heavy to carry. As a West Coast girl, this took a few minutes to problem solve. The easy option would have been to go back to bed. Instead, I shoveled out an opening. Then I grabbed some boots, a charged cell phone for further emergencies, put my baby in a sling, and trudged to school. In some ways, being in a school bubble made my world easier because I only knew my classmates. My family and friends were far away. Where's my baby's father? You will find out in **Month Five.**

☐ **Recap:** How's your world shaping up? Are you working or staying at home? Is your partner helping? Has your partner taken paternity or maternity leave? Have you joined the online baby world? Are you blogging, Facebooking, Snapchatting, sharing your experiences with others in a cyber community? Do you feel like you have the hang of this motherhood thing? Whether you do or you don't, it's "me" time again, so don't forget to focus yourself, too.

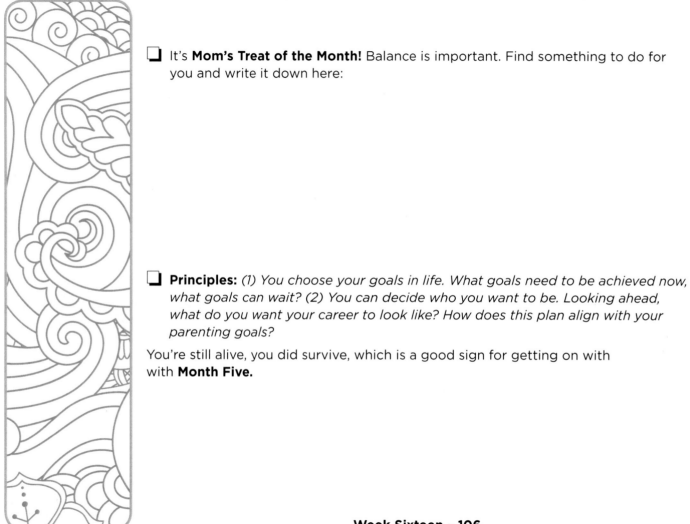

❑ It's **Mom's Treat of the Month!** Balance is important. Find something to do for you and write it down here:

❑ **Principles:** *(1) You choose your goals in life. What goals need to be achieved now, what goals can wait? (2) You can decide who you want to be. Looking ahead, what do you want your career to look like? How does this plan align with your parenting goals?*

You're still alive, you did survive, which is a good sign for getting on with with **Month Five.**

CHAPTER FIVE

Month Five

Week Seventeen—Date

"I just can't get over how much babies really cry. I really had no idea what I was getting into. To tell you the truth, I thought it would be more like getting a cat."

Anne Lamott, *Operating Instructions*

Five ways motherhood isn't what I expected:

1.

2.

3.

4.

5.

"To show a child what has once delighted you, To find the child's delight added to your own, So that there is now double delight seen in the glow of trust and affection... This is happiness."

J.B. Priestley, in *Reader's Digest*

Five ways motherhood is better than I expected:

1.

2.

3.

4.

5.

Tip: Read Anne Lamott's book, *Operating Instructions.* It is a journal about her first year with her son. It's a quick and enjoyable read that might touch your heart.

Week Eighteen—Date

"My friend's doctor says it's okay to give your baby lots of Infant Tylenol® when babies are teething—they need it. It helps them. Oh! He doesn't have any teeth yet?"

Maggie, mother of four

Have any of your ideas about administering Infant Tylenol®, Dimetapp®, etc. to your child changed? If so, why?

How many kids did you plan to have? How many do you want now?

If your child has siblings/cousins, explain how the siblings/cousins interact with your child and why you like or don't like it.

Today I feel passionate about...

Has your baby started to smile at you? Share:

Has your baby started to talk? Share:

Sitting up helps with spitting up. When your baby takes in too much air while feeding, a likely reaction is to spit up—an action that peaks at four months. Try sitting your baby up while feeding, make sure the baby bottle nipple holes are big enough, burp your baby after each feeding, and make sure your baby's clothes aren't too tight and putting pressure on your baby's tummy.

Plan Ahead tip: Arrange for babysitting and cleaning *before* you need them. Best to arrange support while you are still feeling upbeat and able to handle it all—before you are too exhausted, grumpy, and not fun to be around. Plus, if you are on a budget you may even be able to exchange favors if you make arrangements while you are still feeling balanced.

Joke: *Why did the new mom want to make her baby mad? She was hoping he'd give her the silent treatment.*

Week Nineteen—Date

"If you don't have children the longing for them will kill you,
and if you do the worry about them will kill you."

Buchi Emecheta, *The Joys of Motherhood*

The most memorable thing that happened this week was...

Does your baby use a soother? What do you use? ;)

I find I am different now because...

My childless friends don't understand when I can't...

My pet is _____ with my baby because...

I'm grateful for...

If you are on a baby budget here are a few tips:

"I got get rid of all my maternity clothes. I sold them on Facebook sites. I use the local groups, such as 805-trading or 805-baby stuff [their area code]. I have gotten good stuff on there and I've sold good stuff on there. I pick a lowball price, take a picture and people buy it. It's with local people on Facebook, so then you'll meet up in a store or somewhere public and pass this stuff off. You'll put what you're selling in a post, put a price on it, and if people want it they will message you."

Brynn, age 23, working mom on a budget

Maternity clothes and baby clothes can also be sold to consignment stores. Usually, stores give you up to 50% of the profit after the clothes are actually sold. The Salvation Army, Diabetes Association, Big Brothers, and many churches will be happy to take donations. Also, if you live in an apartment building and put up a sign offering free baby clothes, you might be surprised at how many takers there are. Another option is to put a post on Facebook (perhaps a baby group), Instagram, or another form of social media and spread the word you have free clothes to give away.

Joke: *My mother told me to find a husband when in university. She never told me he had to attend.*

Week Twenty—Date

"If men had to have babies, they would only ever have one each."

Princess Diana, in *The Observer*

The most memorable thing that happened this week was...

I would love it if _____ would understand when...

I'm so amazed my child is able to...

I entertain my baby by...

My other friends who have younger children are...

"Go in peace my daughter. And remember that, in a world of ordinary mortals, you are a Wonder Woman."

Queen Hippolyta
***Wonder Women,* TV series**

I/we (circle) have taken our baby to the doctor because...

Note: Although some people like to believe gender discrimination is a relic of the past in developed countries, boys are still preferred and privileged over girls in almost every society and culture. According to a 2011 Gallup poll, if Americans could only have one child, 40% would prefer a boy compared to just 28%, who would prefer to have a girl (Gallup Poll, *States of the World Atlas*).

Checklist

☐ **A Baby-Free Night Out:** Assess whether you have gone out at night and if not, think about making a plan to go out! Try going out after 9 pm for at least an hour. If you can, make an effort not to worry, to be happy, and to enjoy a few minutes out. Trust me, your baby will not remember later. Even if you feel tired when it's time to go, remember once you are out, you will find more energy.

☐ **A Night Out with the Baby:** If you don't want to have a sitter or don't feel comfortable leaving your baby, there are still ways to make it work. Here's Stella's story:

Stella, a first-time mother of twins emphasizes she had no restrictions!

Stella says they went everywhere with her infant twins, she repeats, *"Everywhere!"* She knew her babies would nap two hours so she planned around that. She and her husband even went to dinner with friends.

"I had figured it out. When we were ordering our food and our wine and everything, we would ask to use a to-go plate since we knew we had a limit of two hours. So we would say to the servers that we want the food on a to-go plate but we will eat it here and we want the check at the same time, and as soon as the kids started crying we just locked it up and walked away.

I tell everyone but they don't always understand. They let the kids cry or they take the kids outside for a few minutes, one parent walks out and one doesn't, and they take turns. Even if we were with friends we did the same plan as we did on our own. We would go for a set amount of time. Our friends can have their regular meal and we'll have it with them—and Vladi [her husband] knew the timing. We went to the restaurant on the dot in two-hour increments—we just knew they wake up in two hours. We would leave just before two hours and our friends can stay longer."

❏ **Baby Book:** Take out that baby book and write at least one reason why your kid's awesome. You'll probably find yourself finding enough time to write many more.

❏ **Reassess Your Wardrobe:** Throw out at least one pregnancy outfit, or burn it (safely, please), or donate it. If you decide to have another baby there is no reason to wear an outfit you never liked in the first place. Think fashion forward and there will be new items to wear by then.

☐ **Plan Without Stress:** You may have also discovered by now that everything takes longer. When making plans, schedule your time so that you hope to arrive a half an hour before your anticipated meet-up. If you're a super mom and on time—which will be a miracle by the way—it is still less stressful to give yourself the extra time and plan for the unexpected.

☐ **Keep Details to Yourself:** Often people who are not parents may not want to hear about the little details of your baby's sleep schedule and the ups and downs that make it hard to plan. If you have to give a reason, try to keep it brief. It's one of those things most people might not feel comfortable telling you.

☐ **Feeling blue:** Overall 7.5% of Canadian and one out of seven American moms report depressive symptoms during the In the USA, The bottom line is that smoking and drugs don't help! What does help is finding community; so instead consider joining a group, chat with some new people at the park or a coffee shop, or reach out to a friend (Government of Canada, *JAVAPsychiatry*).

Checklist

- ☐ Give yourself permission to forget stuff.
- ☐ Are you informed about dental care for infants?
- ☐ What are your plans for immunizations?
- ☐ Have you figured out how to take showers without interruptions?
- ☐ If you go to a restaurant do you remember to call ahead to see if they have a high chair?
- ☐ **Baby Schedule Tip:** Does your sleep schedule work for you? The best baby schedule is the one that works for your life.

  "Professionally, I read a ton of parenting books. I feel like I read all of them. One of the things I had stressed a little bit less about was the whole thing about having a schedule. It's good to fall into a schedule, but it's not necessary to fight your kid's natural schedule so much.

  Linda, family counselor, mother of one

- ☐ **Use caution when posting baby photos.** You make your own choices as a parent but you may want to keep tabs on yourself, your baby's father or other parent, and your relatives about posting baby pictures. Consider refraining from posting nude baby pictures online due to predators. In one instance, my friend had no idea her husband had posted an album filled with naked pictures of her newborn baby and her toddler and he had inadvertently posted it on a public setting. Anyone could view it.

Week Twenty-One—Date

"I have often thought what a melancholy world this would be without children; and what an inhuman world without the aged."

Samuel Taylor Coleridge, poet

I felt exhausted/rested (circle) this week because...

Relatives who are really involved with the baby are...

Some of my relatives/people who have not seen the baby yet are _____ because_____.

The spit up phase in my baby's life has ended/not ended (circle). Do tell. ;)

I still want to show the baby to...

I'm grateful for...

Joke: *My mother loves being a grandma. Just give her a chair, some food, and no responsibility.*

You Can Potty Train Your Baby at Five Months, You Just Need a Baby Whisperer!

Kate and her partner are writer and directors who live in Hollywood, Los Angeles, California. Kate had their baby on the cusp of her fortieth birthday. Her partner continued working after the baby was born, and Kate planned to direct a movie when her baby was four months old. She set up a babysitter to take over for her, but as with most things in life events were not going as planned. Here is a film industry mom story:

"My babysitter was great, but she was my friend's daughter and primarily an aspiring actress. Before I hired her, she'd applied to be on a network reality television show, and my thoughts were: 'Oh no, they are going to pick her!' And they did! But she was like, 'Oh, I'm sure I'll get kicked off in time for you to direct the movie.' She went to do the show and I was waiting and waiting and waiting, but she didn't get kicked off and she didn't get kicked off, and she didn't get kicked off. Every day I thought, 'Oh my god, when is she coming back? I have to do this movie!'

When you're on these shows you can't communicate with anybody. You can't be calling them and asking, 'Are you getting kicked off?' or 'What's going on?' Finally, I thought, 'She might win this thing!' [laughs] So I realized, 'I've gotta get somebody else.'"

Work pending—help wanted!

"We bought this house so I'm driving from one side of the city to the other with a little tiny baby and I'm having to talk to the contractors and the house painters and breastfeed at the same time. There's no one helping me because my partner is working so I'm doing all of this stuff by myself and I'm like, 'What am I gonna do? I have no nanny and I'm going to be shooting a movie. What am I gonna do?!'

Then, the greatest thing that happened. Rachel, my partner, was shooting a pilot and one of the producers had kids. The producer said, 'I know a baby nurse for you. However, she can only work for you for three months because after that she's going back to El Salvador. This sounded great because it would give us enough time to find another nanny.

I speak Spanish, but it was a bit rusty. I remember, I picked up the nanny and she was this little short person with a big smile on her face."

The Baby Whisperer

"That night I'm in bed with the baby, or it might have been really early in the morning, and the baby started crying. She came into the bedroom and she basically did this hand motion, 'Give me the baby, give me the baby.' And I said, 'Really?' I gave her the baby and she was just like Mary Poppins. She was so self-sufficient, this woman who didn't speak any English. She was wonderful and confident and she took care of everything.

The other thing is that she could make any baby respond to her. She was like a Baby Whisperer. She would put a pillow on her head and my baby would laugh and laugh. Soon she had him happy and totally content and I thought, 'Thank God, I don't have to worry about him during this filming.'"

Potty training at five months

"As I said, she was a Baby Whisperer. She could communicate with babies. When she first met my baby she said, 'He doesn't understand me yet.' And then later she says, 'Now he understands me.' She was right, he did.

She put him on a schedule where he got up in the morning and was put on the potty, and he would go poop in the potty. He knew the potty was there, and when he needed to go, he would go on the potty."

The nanny, Estrella, managed to teach Kate's five-month old son what to do, by taking him into the bathroom every morning and putting him on the potty. Estrella would make a grunting noise and a face, and eventually this little darling was potty trained at only five months! Kate said she never had to change a poopy diaper after that. What a lucky mama! Please let me tell those of you who are not having such success with this, not all babies are potty trained at five months. It did not happen in our house. Many children start much later.

Potty training: Potty training often doesn't happen until children are age two or older. It's often based on the child being physically and emotionally ready. Here are a few books to help you get prepared:

- ❀ *Once Upon a Potty*®—Alona Frankel (for him or for her) (Board Book: February 2014)
- ❀ *Potty Superhero*—Mabel Forsyth (Paragon Board Books: February 2013)
- ❀ *Potty*—Leslie Patricelli (Candlewick Press Hardcover: September 2014)
- ❀ *Knock! Knock! Who's There?:A Potty Training Picture Book*—Elissambura (Hardcover: March 2017)
- ❀ *I Use the Potty*—Maria van Lieshout (Hardcover: March 2016)
- ❀ *My Thomas Potty Book* (Thomas & Friends) (Random House Board Book: January 2016)
- ❀ *Girls' Potty Time*—Dawn Sirett (Publishing DK Board Book: February 2010)
- ❀ *My Big Boy Potty*—Joanna Cole (Hardcover: December 2004)

Month in Review

You've made it to the **fifth month.** You're almost over the half a year hump, so you can handle whatever comes your way. You're stronger than ever. In **month five,** my son's dad came for a visit. Since his job as a management consultant took him out-of-town most weekdays and we were not sure of our future, he had stayed behind during the move back East. However, we were still technically together. While he was in our world for a few days, his time consisted of helping me with my homework more than helping with the baby, arguing, and having a few fun meals out. Yet, as with all things in life, we were figuring it out. My baby, on the other hand, had become a superstar crawler at only four months. By five months, he was shocking the students on the East Coast with his speed crawling. I was managing to keep up with the school work and thrilled that the end of school was around the corner.

❏ **Recap:** Have you gone on a date night? How is your sleep schedule working? Is your child teething/crawling/not crawling/talking? How involved are relatives and friends involved in your parenting life? How's your fitness routine going? Is your body getting back into shape?

❏ **Mom's Treat of the Month:** Life doesn't always go as planned, but sometimes it does! You've made it over the five-month mark and are on to **month six!** Half a year is coming up. Time to recharge and take out a few moments for **Mom's Treat of the Month.** Write it here:

❏ **Principles:** *(1) All babies are unique. Everyone has different milestones. Some will be ahead of the curve and some will be behind. (2) Sometimes there's this notion that when you have a baby life will stop, but it keeps moving forward. In order to keep moving forward along with it, you have to learn to juggle, think outside the box, and be open to new ideas! (3) Share your experiences so other people can help you and offer solutions.*

Think forward motion heading into **Month Six.**

What I want to remember...

CHAPTER SIX

Month Six

Week Twenty-Two—Date

"A man finds out what is meant by a spitting image when he tries to feed cereal to his infant."

Imogene Fey in Jilly Cooper and Tom Hartman, *Violets and Vinegar*

Sanity Tip

Sometimes having my baby with me is a better way to de-stress than having a babysitter. *"Since I have a hard time turning off the worrying, sometimes actually cuddling with my baby and having her right there is very comforting for me, so I might take a couple of days where we go off on our own."*

Janelle, age 23

The funniest things my child did this week were...

When I think about childcare, I think it is best to...

If someone were to ask me about my child's other parent, I would say...

Romance in my life has changed for...

Teething is...

If I do a vision board, the first thing I'm going to put on it is...

Exercise Tips: Try listening to a book or music or watching your favorite TV program while on a bike, treadmill or elliptical. This can change your perspective and help you look forward to an hour of focused entertainment. You can also try working out with someone who is in better shape than you. By doing this, you can see what they do, learn their routine, and then modify it for your own workout. This can help you stretch your goals and your mindset.

Week Twenty-Three—Date

"Seems to be the basic conflict between men and women, sexually is that men are like firemen. To us, sex is an emergency and no matter what we're doing we can be ready in two minutes. Women, on the other hand, are like fire. They're very exciting, but the conditions have to be exactly right for it to occur."

Jerry Seinfeld, comedian

When I think about romance, I feel...

I love my partner, but...

How big will our family be?

Have you decided when and if you're going to have another baby?

Who is dressing cuter these days, you or your baby? ;)

What is your baby's cutest outfit? What's yours?

Tip: If your relationship needs a shot of romance try going to an action flick. A study suggests couples can misinterpret adrenaline jolts as sexual excitement toward each other (*Ladies' Home Journal*).

Joke: *People say it takes half the length of your average relationship to get over it. I thought this is fantastic. At this rate, I'll have a new boyfriend by tomorrow.*

Week Twenty-Four—Date

"The smile you give is the smile you get back." Goldie Hawn, actress

"Babies are a nice way to start people." Don Herold, *There Ought to be a Law*

I feel like I am spending quality time with my child when we...

There are a couple of things I feel I'm doing right, such as...

My child's favorite book/song is...

As far as my career goes...

Note: Approximately one out of five people in Canada are personally affected by adoption in some way (Adoption Council of Canada). They may be adopted themselves, or be related to people through adoption, or have birth relatives who were adopted. That equates to about seven million Canadians affected by adoption in 2017 (Adoption Council of Canada). Even so, adoptive parents receive only 35 weeks of parental leave in Canada, compared to a total of 50 weeks for biological parents. The extra 15 weeks are designated for the biological mother during pregnancy, but the Adoption Council of Canada argues adoptive parents should have the same amount of parental leave as biological parents due to the unique stresses and difficulties of the process.

Adoption

There are various definitions of adoption, from the legal definition to living with a family that isn't your own or living with an extended family member(s). For our purposes we are using a flexible definition.

> *"My husband and I went to China to adopt our daughter, who was 13 months old when I was 46. Many people had been telling me I was too old to get into being a mother at that stage of my life, and I'm so happy I paid them no heed. I have loved raising Zhi (we kept her Chinese name), who is a wonderful person—smart, affectionate, creative, musical, very loving and beautiful."*
>
> **Patricia,** Toronto, Ontario

A sampling of famous people who were adopted:

John Lennon, Marilyn Monroe, Kristin Chenoweth, Ingrid Bergman, Nelson Mandela, Babe Ruth, Michael Bay, Priscilla Presley, Melissa Gilbert, Ray Liotta, Jesse Jackson, Sarah McLachlan, Truman Capote, Richard Burton, Frances McDormand, Faith Hill, Steve Jobs, Edgar Allan Poe, Jamie Foxx, Eleanor Roosevelt, Ted Danson, Nancy Reagan, Nicole Richie, and many more.

A sampling of famous people who have adopted:

Sandra Bullock, Charlize Theron, Rosie O'Donnell, Madonna, Angelina Jolie, Brad Pitt, Tom Cruise, Robert Munsch, Woody Allen, Kirstie Alley, Loni Anderson, Julie Andrews, George Burns, Kirk Cameron, Magic Johnson, Diane Keaton, David Kelly, Nicole Kidman, Willie Mays, Frances McDormand, Ewan McGregor, Oscar de la Renta, John Denver, Walt Disney, Edie Falco, Marie Osmond, Hugh Jackman, Katherine Heigl, Steven Spielberg, Barbara Walters, Nia Vardalos, and many more.

Joke: *I think my adoption agency has some explaining to do. Given that the six-month-old we adopted is potty trained, makes his own breakfast, and is 4'3"!*

Week Twenty-Five—Date

"I feel like I'm babysitting in the Twilight Zone. I keep waiting for the parents to show up because we are out of chips and Diet Coke."

Anne Lamott, *Operating Instructions*

I have to make time for...

A whole weekend away from my child would mean...

The cause: My baby's teething. The effect:

The weather affects our life because...

Babies and Artificial Light

"I try to keep the lights on during the day and turn them down at night to show her the difference between night and day."

Janelle, 23, first-time mom

"We put blackout blinds in the baby's room for when he slept at night."

Linda, age 46, first-time mom

It turns out Janelle and Linda's instincts are correct. According to the American Sleep Association, babies are not born with a concept of day or night since the womb is always dark. It turns out that light suppresses the production of melatonin (the naturally occurring hormone that promotes sleep) almost twice as much in babies as it does in adults. This means it's much harder for babies to fall asleep in light compared to grownups (*Journal of Clinical Endocrinology & Metabolism*). It may be worthwhile to keep the light low during diaper changes when you are hoping to put your baby back to sleep. There was some concern that nightlights might cause nearsightedness, but it turns out it's genetics. Children whose parents are nearsighted, are more likely to be nearsighted. It's not because of the lighting.

Joke: *What do you call a baby goat who sleeps during the day?* "A
  A kid napper.

Week Twenty-Six—Date

"Motherhood isn't easy or men would do it."

Dorothy, character on *The Golden Girls*

Most memorable thing that happened this week was...

My child's horoscope sign/rising sign/Chinese zodiac year is...

We seem a little similar because...

We seem a little different because...

My baby reminds me of the father because...

I'm grateful for...

Fun Fact: In 1980, popular band, Salt-n-Pepa, consisted of all single mothers at the time their successful singles "Shoop" and "Whatta Man" propelled their album *Very Necessary* to sell over five million copies worldwide.

When asked about celebrity motherhood, Salty (Cheryl James) said, *"It has deepened our spiritual faith and I hope we'll continue to follow God's plan for us."*

My Opinion

I would prefer the terms "independent parent" or "independent mother," particularly when a so-called single mother is in a relationship or is the primary person paying the bills for her family.

Janelle—Listening to Yourself

"So many people are telling you all kinds of different things, and there is a certain amount of mommy shaming and judgment, especially if you are looking online and you can't see each other face to face. People are not so nice to each other, but I think it's really important to try your best to have confidence in what you're doing. As long as your baby is healthy, happy and growing then you must be doing something right and it's not always going to be what other people tell you to do."

Janelle, age 23,

Joke: *I'm trying to trust my own inner voice. It's just really hard to decide which one.*

New Mom's Favorite Baby Gadgets

"A bunch of the women from the church we grew up in pitched in and got us a car seat, so that was really great."

Janelle, age 23

"Baby Bjorn®! You don't have to get the Baby Bjorn®, whatever is comfortable for you, but I use it all the time to carry her."

Kara, age 27

"The UPPAbaby bassinet®. I highly recommend people get a bassinet stroller. I loved that thing. For one thing he would nap in the stroller. He wouldn't go down for a nap, so we would walk him around the house. We created a little circuit inside the house. It's not a very big house, but we would sing a song, and do loops around the house pushing the UPPAbaby® stroller and letting him nap in the stroller."

Linda, age 45

"The many Medela Breast Pumps®. Number One. Medela Swing® is my on-the-go pump. I never plugged it in, I only used it with batteries—clips easily to pocket or waistband and is well hidden with a flowy shirt top. Number Two. The Medela Pump in Style®. This is my daily friend. The one I take to work (I have often left it there for the week) and I also used it in the car with a car adaptor plug. Many people notice that the pumping noise starts to sound like little messages. Very funny, and makes you feel a little crazy. Number Three. Medela Hospital Grade Breast Pump®. It's bringing out the big guns. If you're looking to provide breast milk for a whole year, it means counting ounces and watching your diet and doing anything you can to

maintain your supply. I bought this at nine months and kept it until 15 months just to use at night and on the weekends, so I could get that little bit more."

Dee-Dee, age 47

"His Bumbo® seat! He would sit in the middle of the table in his Bumbo seat."

Linda S., age 46

Joke: *Why did the au pair sit in the baby's seat after she ate brownies? She thought she was supposed to sit in the high chair.*

Month in Review

Wow! It's really here. **Half-year** birthday celebration time. Are you still labeling your child's age by months? In my universe, it was an early start to summer. I was very excited because I had completed my second university degree and was heading from the East Coast back to the West Coast. It was time for a new chapter. My son was crawling and reaching various baby milestones. It was time for his dad to take his paternity leave and for me to jump into the working world. I was going to be a segment producer for a TV show.

It was also time for me to enjoy my special treat of the month. My friend's older brother had a role in a movie that was recently released and I didn't have a sitter. I wanted to see the movie so I planned it all out. I knew when my baby would be asleep. I kept a baby bottle on hand in case he woke up. I bundled him up with a fleece hat with ear flaps, put him in a sling, and bought a ticket to the matinee showing at a movie theater nearby. There was no one in the balcony. I knew I would have to leave if my baby woke up or made noise but he didn't, and I spent two blissful hours watching a movie in the middle of the day.

❑ **Recap:** Has your baby started to crawl? Has your baby started to murmur something you can understand? Have you traveled at all or left your child for a little longer than before? Have you changed your baby's sleeping schedule? Have you figured out your childcare for now and the upcoming future? If you're transitioning from breastfeeding to bottles have you worked it out?

❏ **Half a year—check!** They grow up so fast. Only another 17 and a half years to go, with the exception of summer camp or boarding school options. ;) I hope you will leap into month seven after enjoying your **Mom's Treat of the Month.** It's important to write it down so it happens. It's not just planning it out, you know you are going to take action. You can control the little things. Please write what you did for yourself here:

❏ **Principles:** *(1) There are so many modern products out on the market to assist new moms. Explore your options. (2) When choosing new companies, consider researching to see if they do animal testing, and whether they choose to use ingredients and materials that are in the best interest of your environment and your body.*

The love your baby exudes towards you feels like heaven. Nothing is so pure. Enjoy a hug and dance spin with your little one and leap into **Month Seven.**

CHAPTER SEVEN

Month Seven

Week Twenty-Seven—Date

"It's a mystery to me why adults expect perfection from children. Few grownups can get through a whole day without making a mistake."

Marlene Cox, in *Ladies' Home Journal*

My relationship with my child's other parent is different than before because...

What do you miss from your single life?

What is so much better now?

I feel like I am communicating better with my baby because...

Do you believe in having a baby monitor?

Have you decided if you want to create traditions for your child? What are some that are important to you?

Where do you want to spend major holidays? Why?

Dental Tip: The American Dental Association recommends starting proper dental care right from your baby's first tooth. Otherwise, uninformed parents could find themselves with a 10-month-old baby with a cavity. It is not safe for babies to play with a toothbrush on their own, but parents can brush their teeth with a dry toothbrush. Then, try using water or infant toothpaste until children are six years old. Regular toothpaste may be too abrasive.

Baby Teeth: Babies are born with 20 of their primary teeth, which typically start to appear when a baby is approximately five to eight months old. It's important that babies hold on to their baby teeth as long as possible so that their permanent teeth don't drift into the wrong spot! This can cause overcrowding and crooked teeth. Both the American and Canadian Dental Associations advise bringing your baby to the dentist by their first birthday.

Teething Tip

"When my son was teething I gave him a frozen waffle."

Amber, age 27

Week Twenty-Eight—Date

"Children think not what is past, nor what is to come, but enjoy the present which few of us do."

Jean de la Bruyere, *The Works of Mons. De La Bruyere*

Watching my child sit up makes me feel...

Dealing with my child's relatives is...

When other people take care of my baby I...

Is it a challenge to let other people watch your baby?

The longest sleep I had this week was...

Who is smiling more this week? You or your baby?

What is the funniest thing anyone in your house said this week?

Baby-Proofing Tips: You can reduce stress by avoiding situations where babies can get hurt. Make sure to put your baby on surfaces that are low to the ground. As a new mom, when my baby first started moving on his own, he rolled right off a chair. Another time, his baby seat vibrated itself right off a counter—luckily he was seat-belted in so his head didn't make any contact with the floor. Woops. Here are a few baby-proofing products to start you off: *Skip Hop Moby Bath Spout Universal Fit®, Blue, Safety 1st Pinch Guard®.* Some others you might consider are sharp table corner guards, outlet covers, door knob locks, and more.

"One of the first things a child learns in a healthy family is trust."
Mr. Rogers, TV personality

More Baby Safety Tips: It's helpful to have no slip bath mats. Never leave your baby unattended in the bathtub, even for a few seconds. Protect your child near stoves and windows. Don't leave toys in the crib when your child is sleeping. There's more, please research!

Week Twenty-Nine—Date

"Young girls are told you have to be the delicate princess. Hermione taught you that you can be the warrior."

Emma Watson, actress

"Love has nothing to do with what you are expecting to get—only with what you are expecting to give—which is everything."

Katharine Hepburn, actress

My child's favorite baby friend is...

My favorite baby friend of my child is...

When I find it hard to get anything accomplished, I remember it is easier when...

I'm proud of my child's sleep schedule because...

The sleep schedule has improved from a few months ago because...

My baby and her grandparents...

Object Permanence: Do you find your baby loves to throw things out of the crib and then want it back again? Usually between four and seven months children learn that when something leaves their view, it isn't completely gone. You might find that your child is having a lot of fun with this new understanding.

Fact: In 2015, 82% of US births were by millennial women who themselves were born between 1981 and 1997. By 2015, more than 16 million millennial females in the US had given birth, according to the National Center for Health Statistics.

Joke: *What do you call a baby that whines about everything?*
A crybaby.

Week Thirty—Date

"I wear my bra 24 hours a day now. I've lost my butt and gained a tummy. I'm sick of breastfeeding. I want my body back now!"

Nicky, married mother of two

Our biggest milestone this week was...

My child is capable of many things, including...

In order to help my child's development, my child is attending...

My child's appearance has changed now because...

My appearance has changed now because...

I'm grateful for...

Baby classes: Gymboree Play and Music Programs are available across North America. You can find classes for your newborn at www.gymboreeclasses.com. The age groups are arranged into levels. Play and Learn 1 is for babies zero to six months old. Play and Learn 2 is for children six to 10 months old. Play and Learn 3 is for children age 10 to 16 months. There is also a Baby Lab for children age zero to 10 months old. Other choices include Musikgarten (1-800-216-6864 or www.musikgarten.org). These classes focus on how to integrate music into your child's life, including classes for zero to 18 months that are designed for parents to enjoy with their newborns. Swim classes are another good idea. Many YMCAs offer them: www.ymca.net. Public libraries have story hours. There are also Mommy and Me groups that are held at community centers and churches. Usually these groups allow time for mothers to share their views.

FYI: In 2018, the Gerber baby campaign chose 18-month-old Lucas Warren, from Dalton, Georgia, as their spokesperson. Each year approximately 6,000 (one in 700 babies) are born with Down syndrome in the United States. Just like baby Lucas, everyone has the potential to do exciting things!

Week Thirty-One—Date

"A man who has been the indisputable favorite of his mother keeps for life the feeling of a conqueror, that confidence of success often induces real success."

Sigmund Freud, neurologist

My favorite way to spend time with my child is...

I wish someone had told me...

My body/hair/eyes (circle) are better now because...

Who has the cuter hairstyle this week? You or your baby? ;)

I'm really trying to overcome...

I'm grateful for...

Tip: If you think you are your mother's favorite child, don't be so sure. A pilot study conducted by Cornell University and Louisiana State University found that most adults with siblings believe themselves to be their mom's favorite. The study also found out 59% of the time, the study subjects were wrong!

Crawling

Babies tend to crawl by eight months. In 1994, the US launched a "Back to Sleep" campaign initiated to promote babies sleeping on their back to avoid sudden infant death syndrome (SIDS). As the number one cause of baby deaths in the first year, SIDS has decreased 50% since the campaign began. It's now called, "Safe to Sleep." An unexpected side effect is that many babies who sleep on their backs are skipping the crawling stage and going straight to walking. Babies may like sleeping on their back because they don't have to roll over to see what's everyone's up to, they can just open their eyes. US babies who sleep on their back are up to over 70% from 20% before the campaign. It is also important babies spend time on their stomachs during daylight hours to develop other motor skills and to avoid flat spots on their head (AAP, NIH, Mayo).

Joke: *My baby's so fast he won a crawling contest at nine months. Wow, that's amazing! What did he win? Knee pads.*

Hindsight

"I recommend getting help in the first six months even if you have to pay. I would not save that money. That money needs to go to your sanity to have somebody there— even just a nanny during the day or at night—if you don't have family to help. You can always make more money later on, but your sanity is more important in those first six months when I would say it is the hardest."

Kati, age 37, married mother of twins plus an older child

"I wish I was more educated on the postpartum period and the getting your life back period which is a lot more stressful than labor."

Sarah, age 27, mother of one

"Next time, I would not recruit so many relatives to be at the birth. Instead, I would enjoy their support a few days after the baby was born when I was not so exhausted."

Aubrey, age 42, mother of one

"If you are splitting up with your partner, my advice is to register legally right away. I know mediation is superior but get your ducks in a line before you run out of money, before you unexpectedly lose your job, and before your find yourself in a helpless position."

Jen, age 27 mother of one

"When I found out I was pregnant, I didn't realize how much I would want to talk to my mom, find out her techniques and stuff."

Janelle, age 23, whose mother passed away when Janelle was 18 years old

"I did not anticipate how emotional my baby's little milestones were going to be for me and how quickly it was going to go. Everyone says, 'Oh it flies by, it flies by'...and it definitely flies by. It's the little things like she's never had a bottle—and we're in the process of reworking her schedule as far as breastfeeding goes, we're trying to take it down a little—and that's been really emotional for me, you know."

Kara, age 27, mother of one

Joke: *What happened to the strange boy who grew eyes on his butt?*
He gained hindsight. Kid joke created by my son Callam at age 9.

Month in Review

Now you are a baby expert! It's **month seven.** You've changed diapers, fed the baby, figured out immunizations and dental care. Your baby might be playing with object permanence and enjoying games like peekaboo. Your baby might be crawling around everywhere, but don't fret if not. Many babies wait until later or skip it altogether. One mother said, *"He started crawling at nine months and walking at a year almost to the day."*

You have learned more about yourself and your family and what schedule works for you. Looking back, rejoice over the giant learning cycle you've been through and how much more you understand now—about parenting, babies, and relationships.

My baby's father found handling paternity a little tougher than he imagined. I would be at my office (which was literally surrounded by windows) and I would see him holding up our child through the glass pleading for me to come out of my office and take him. I'm guessing he knew I would be won over by our child's cuteness. At one point we went for lunch and had a picnic in the grass. He had a teary mini-meltdown—the dad, not our baby—who was oblivious and enjoying his new teething toy. I gave him—the dad—a pat on the back, some words of encouragement, and went back to work. We all have our parenting learning curves! His paternity leave was three months in Canada and I was going to make the most of it. Talking to my grownup co-workers felt like a treat. It was only a short-term job position with short days, so I was lucky.

❏ **Recap:** You have fast become a baby expert. Looking back, remember when you had no idea how many hours a baby slept? Do you recall the days when you wondered how it would be to change diapers and how often? You are a relationship expert now, too. Before you may have wondered how people close to you would react to the baby. By now, you have watched the other parent or person closest to you and how they are with the baby. These mysteries have been solved. What baby gadgets have been lifesavers? Is your baby eating any solid food? What milestones has your baby made? What advice would you impart to new moms? Now that you have gone from novice to expert. What have you learned?

❑ **Mom's Treat of the Month:** I know, I know. Your baby is so darn cute! It's hard to be away from your little pumpkin. Or maybe you feel someone else needs the time away from the baby more than you? Stop right there! Don't wait, you'll need the strength for **month eight.** You deserve some mom's special time: spa anyone? If you are on a budget, there are ways to do this cheaply—did someone whisper, Groupon? There's no reason not to eat at home a little more, make your own coffee a little more, if that's what it takes to afford a blowout, a massage, or a manicure. You can also try visiting a new place. It doesn't have to be far. Go for a hike or walk in a place with new scenery. Please write your **Mom's Treat of the Month here:**

❑ **Principles:** *(1) Change with the times. Modern science and research comes up with new ideas for raising babies all the time so look online! (2) Just because you need extra help right now, doesn't mean you will later, so treat yourself to as much support as possible.*

It's never too late to start feeling great; here's to having a super **Month Eight!**

What I want to remember...

CHAPTER EIGHT

Month Eight

Week Thirty-Two—Date

"I love my child with all my heart but let's not pretend it's easy. Every time we're out my husband keeps telling everyone how great it is and I feel like an ogre."

Danielle, mother of one

What system do you need to put in place to make your life a little simpler?

I'm looking forward to...

In order to keep my house clean I...

My thoughts for putting my child in the car to go places is that it's...

What block of time should you allot for your "to do" list?

What miracle do you feel you accomplished this week?

Are you reading to your baby?

"The biggest thing is that I nursed my daughter India until she was 20 months old. I was so excited to be a nursing mom but I did not expect it to be so much work. You have to be really dedicated. I was a really busy person. I had worked full-time always. I like to be busy. When you nurse a baby, you have to take the time and be quiet. It was really a hard transition for me at first because I'm not like that." **Emily,** married mother of one

Planning Tip: Often creating a list of goals for the week is easier and more satisfying than planning what you want to accomplish in a day. I learned this tip from the famous book, *The 7 Habits of Highly Effective People*®, by Stephen R. Covey.

Precious Moments: There's a scene in the movie, *Daddy Day Care* when after a long day's work, the mom (Regina King) comes home to a super messy house. It was her hubby's first day of running a daycare (Eddie Murphy). Under her breath, she says, "*I'm not cleaning this up.*" Then, she goes upstairs to scold them but before she does, she sees her toddler and her hubby (the baby's daddy) asleep on the bed, with a bedtime story still open on top of her husband's lap. Does she yell at them? No. Instead, she sighs and turns off the lights. Sometimes, it's best to have patience with parenting and partners.

Looking for a Family Movie? Try One of These:

- ☐ *Daddy Day Care*—Eddie Murphy, Jeff Garlin, Regina King
- ☐ *Boss Baby*—Alec Baldwin (animated)
- ☐ *Stork Journey*—Shannon Conley (animated)
- ☐ *Paddington Bear 1*—Montgomery Clyde (animated, creator Paul King)
- ☐ *Paddington Bear 2*—Hugh Grant (animated)
- ☐ *Ratatouille*—Brad Garrett (animated, creators Brad Bird and Jan Pinkava)
- ☐ *The Incredibles or Incredibles 2*—Craig T. Nelson (animated, creator Brad Bird)
- ☐ *Heidi* (1937) or *The Little Princess* (1939)—Shirley Temple

Week Thirty-Three—Date

"It sometimes happens, even in the best of families, that a baby is born. This is not necessarily cause for alarm. The important thing is to keep your wits about you and borrow some money."

Elinor Goulding Smith, *The Complete Book of Absolutely Perfect Baby and Child Care*

My favorite way to pamper myself is...

I wish my child would stop...

"We've been having a good time, so the girls are having a good time. Our baby girls are a couple of months apart so they have been playing together, it's been great. It's been nice having a partner."
Angie's friend Kara, is visiting her in LA from San Diego, while Kara's husband is deployed in the military. They met when they were both pregnant in prenatal yoga.

I couldn't have made it through the week if it weren't for the help of...

My favorite way to spend time by myself is...

My baby is so cute when...

If I could have more time in the day, I would...

If you could have one superpower right now what would it be?

Checklist

Travel Gadgets for You and Baby to Make Your Life Easier:

❏ Bottle that heats up in 60 seconds for the plane—the yoomi® bottle: www.yoomi.com.

❏ While you are looking at that bottle you may want to check out the Comotomo™ Natural Feel Baby Bottle: www.comotomo.com.

❏ One non-disposable diaper for emergencies: www.diapers.com

❏ Travel cribs: Call ahead, hotels usually have them. You might be able to save the cost of buying one by calling ahead. Remember less is more.

❏ Travel bassinet for zero to six-month-old babies, try phil&teds Nest™ Compact Bag.

❏ Lotus® Travel Crib and Portable Baby Play Yard or a Baby Bjorn® travel crib.

❏ UPPAbaby® Cruz Travel Bag. When checking your stroller at the airport you can put it in this bag.

❏ A fleece hat with ear flaps to cover ears can come in handy to block out noise, and warm your baby's head if needed.

❏ Bring extra plastic bags and disinfectant wipes.

❏ If you are one of those finicky people you may delight in a Planet Wise™ Wet/Dry bag to help separate wet and dry items: planetwiseinc.com

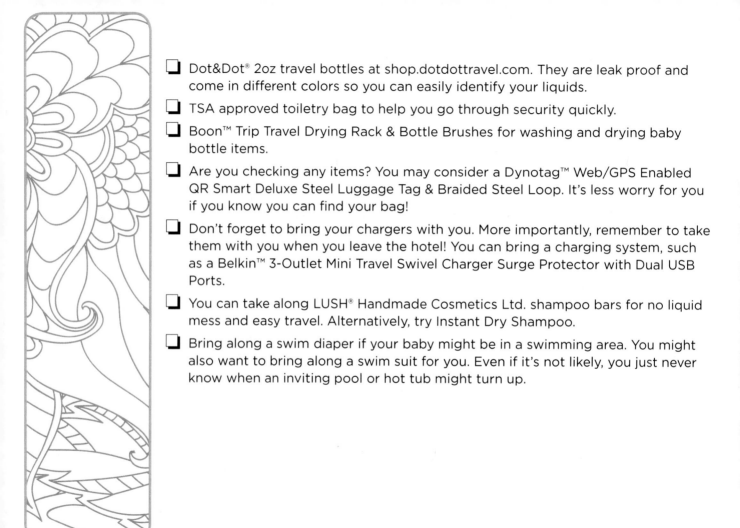

- ❏ Dot&Dot® 2oz travel bottles at shop.dotdottravel.com. They are leak proof and come in different colors so you can easily identify your liquids.

- ❏ TSA approved toiletry bag to help you go through security quickly.

- ❏ Boon™ Trip Travel Drying Rack & Bottle Brushes for washing and drying baby bottle items.

- ❏ Are you checking any items? You may consider a Dynotag™ Web/GPS Enabled QR Smart Deluxe Steel Luggage Tag & Braided Steel Loop. It's less worry for you if you know you can find your bag!

- ❏ Don't forget to bring your chargers with you. More importantly, remember to take them with you when you leave the hotel! You can bring a charging system, such as a Belkin™ 3-Outlet Mini Travel Swivel Charger Surge Protector with Dual USB Ports.

- ❏ You can take along LUSH® Handmade Cosmetics Ltd. shampoo bars for no liquid mess and easy travel. Alternatively, try Instant Dry Shampoo.

- ❏ Bring along a swim diaper if your baby might be in a swimming area. You might also want to bring along a swim suit for you. Even if it's not likely, you just never know when an inviting pool or hot tub might turn up.

Week Thirty-Four—Date

"Motherhood—an accident, an occupation, or a career."

Mary C. Beasley, Commissioner

The most memorable thing that happened this week was...

Sometimes I don't feel I'm very good as a mother because...

In the future, I want...

What is the craziest outfit you have found yourself putting your baby in?

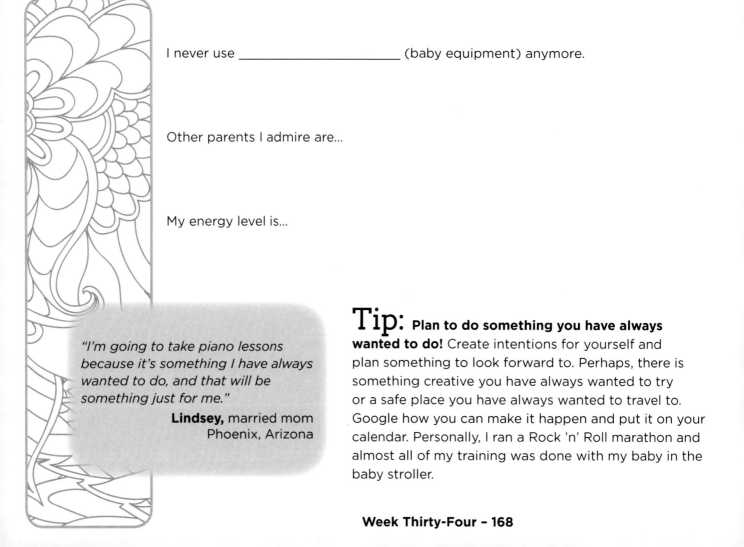

I never use _____ (baby equipment) anymore.

Other parents I admire are...

My energy level is...

"I'm going to take piano lessons because it's something I have always wanted to do, and that will be something just for me."

Lindsey, married mom
Phoenix, Arizona

Tip: **Plan to do something you have always wanted to do!** Create intentions for yourself and plan something to look forward to. Perhaps, there is something creative you have always wanted to try or a safe place you have always wanted to travel to. Google how you can make it happen and put it on your calendar. Personally, I ran a Rock 'n' Roll marathon and almost all of my training was done with my baby in the baby stroller.

Week Thirty-Five—Date

"Accept who you are, unless you are a serial killer."
Ellen DeGeneres, comedian

The best phone call I received this week was from...

The funniest thing my child said this week was...

I love my partner when....

"Becoming parents was the best thing we ever did. It's getting to see the world through the eyes of this child. It sure keeps us young."

Linda, age 46
Bend, Oregon

Mood of the week (draw it):

I have/haven't (circle) made it out of the house at night and it's okay becau fse...

I'm going to give myself a time frame for finishing...

Month in Review

Month eight already! For me, I really learned how time-consuming babies can be. I enjoyed the challenge of finding interesting ways to spend our free time so that we could both experience something new and enjoy our day. Now that my baby could sit up, I joined Gymboree classes. I had bought a jogging stroller, so I could run with the baby. I loved taking my baby to the little indoor wading pool at the public pool. There was also a children's center in Vancouver where parents and babies could go and hang out. It had an activity center, an area where they read to children and even provided parents with free coffee.

❑ **Recap:** What did you accomplish this month? What gadgets have you bought to make your life easier? Who has come to the rescue this month? Have you made sure to ask for help? How are you staying connected to the outside world? If you are a working mom, are you finding quality time with your child?

❑ **Mom's Treat of the Month:** You have made it to **month eight** and you're doing great. What can you do for yourself this month? Treat yourself to some exercise! A tennis match, a hike, volleyball, a yoga class. Try some type of exercise date that includes another grownup human. Write your treat here:

❏ **Principles:** *(1) Don't stress over the little things. (2) Have trust in yourself, your family, and your child. Give them the benefit of the doubt. (3) Be trustworthy so your child can trust you to keep them safe whether at home or traveling.*

I'm sure you're doing just fine, let's see what's going to happen in **Month Nine!**

CHAPTER NINE

Month Nine

Week Thirty-Six—Date

"Children are our most valuable resource."

Herbert Hoover, *The New York Times*, October 21, 1964

Have you thought anymore about traditions? Where do you want to be for holidays?

My child's appearance has changed so much, because...

In order to help my child's development, I'm...

If I could do anything today, I would...

I feel so lucky when...

My child is able to crawl/walk (circle) and he/she communicates with me now by
_____ so our relationship is becoming...

Diaper Changing Tip: Are you practically tackling your child in order to change a diaper? If you are, you might try standing up your baby as you start the process. It may be much easier. But make sure when you are finished wiping to quickly lay him/her down to make sure you aren't missing any spots before standing him/her up again and putting on the diaper.

Note: Globally some 65% of women with primary education or less are married as children, compared with 5% of women who finish high school according to a paper called *Voice and Agency: Empowering Women and Girls for Shared Prosperity.*

Week Thirty-Seven—Date

"Love doesn't make the world go round. Love is what makes the ride worthwhile."

Franklin P. Jones, *The New Beacon Book of Quotations*

The most memorable thing that happened this week was...

I find spending time with the whole family has a different dynamic than when I spend time alone with my child because...

Are you creating time for romance?

My dream weekend right now would be...

My baby gets along with...

What's your baby's cutest outfit these days? Where did you get it?

Sally—Dealing with Childless Friends

Sally says it's been difficult because she and her husband haven't always been able to plan things well enough. She says, *"Sometimes we know we disappoint our friends. We get invited to things and we can't go, and there's this stress of, 'Oh, we're letting our friends down, and we've just bailed on another party or we've just bailed on whatever plans there are.' Especially with the friends that don't have kids, because the friends that do have kids totally understand. It's the people not sharing this journey with us, you know, who are watching but not as participants in the same realm, they don't understand. They might sometimes—it depends on the person.*

I know that some of our friends have made comments to my husband. One time my husband had a plan to go surfing with one of his buddies, but he didn't get enough sleep the night before and he just didn't have it in him to go surfing.

The next time he said he wanted to go with his friends, his friend made a comment to him saying, 'Oh well, we're not going to hold our breath because we know how it is, how you always bail all the time.' I just kind of watched his expression. It was as if his friend was saying he was a flaker. If he really knew my husband, he is FAR from being a flaker. Once he makes a commitment, normally it's in stone, but you need some leeway when you have these little ones that depend on you. You have these responsibilities and it's nice to be able to forgive yourself and just kind of release that pressure. It bothered my husband to no end. And I told him, 'Your friends clearly don't understand but it's not fair for you to hold onto feeling bad,' because it really just put him in a bad mood for the rest of the day."

Tip:
Need a social activity to do with your childless friends? Try going wine-tasting! You can plan the visit for your child's nap time. Of course, don't do the driving yourself, and keep things in moderation, but go and enjoy the ambiance,. Maybe organize a picnic in the grass afterwards, weather permitting. I'm not advocating drinking too much, please be responsible. While you're there, you might want to pick up a little bottle of *Wine Away*™— wine stain remover, just in case your little one bumps into you while you have a glass of wine in your hand in the future. ;)

Joke:
I didn't go into debt when I had children. I just bought a lifetime supply of Charles Shaw.

Week Thirty-Eight—Date

Sweet dreams, form a shade
O'er my lovely infant's head;
Sweet dreams of pleasant streams
Be happy, silent, moony beams.
Sweet sleep, with soft brown
Weave thy brows an infant crown.
Sweet sleep, Angel mild,
Hover o'er my happy child.
                William Blake, "A Cradle Song"

The most memorable thing that happened this week was...

My biggest fear is...

My thoughts about having more children these days are...

Did you send all the thank you cards for your baby showers?

What cities/places have you lived since you became a mom?

Keep trying new healthy foods. If you're having trouble getting your baby to eat your baby-friendly fruits and vegetables, keep trying! As long as the baby's still hungry, you may find it easier while your baby is little to encourage them to adjust to new tastes and textures. You can also combine foods, blend them, and disguise them. Remember, it can take trying a food 10 or more times before your baby starts to like it!

Joke: *Why did the pirate need a map to find the treasure? He was clueless.*
Kid joke by my son Callam.

Paid Maternity Leave

The United States is one of the only countries not to mandate some kind of paid maternity leave for mothers. The other three are Papua New Guinea, Lesotho, and Suriname (*ABC News,* Pew Research Center).

The US Family and Medical Leave Act (FMLA) ensures up to 12 weeks of unpaid maternity leave without fear of job loss for mothers of newly born and adoptive children in companies with greater than 50 employees, but this benefit does not extend to mothers who work for smaller companies. There is also a growing number of companies that will give a week or more of paid paternity and adoptive parent leave (US Dept. of Labor).

In 2018, New York will join California, Rhode Island, and New Jersey as the only states with paid maternity leave mandates (but the time periods are short—four to six weeks and it is for only a partial income replacement).

In 2018, **Canada** is commencing a plan where parents can take up to 18 months leave with some paid benefits, and mothers may start maternity up to 12 weeks before the baby is born (up from the previous option of four weeks). For parents who want a full year and a half, it means stretching the benefits out, not more benefits. You also will have had to work a minimum of 600 hours in the previous year before taking the leave *(The Globe and Mail)*.

Maternity leave in Canada is a combination of maternity leave and parental leave (which means using unemployment insurance benefits) that you get automatically by having a job prior to pregnancy. As people who are working and being employees prior to becoming pregnant, parents are paying a portion of their paycheck to provide for these Unemployment Insurance benefits when they have families. Parental leave can be used by either parent or split between them (Govt. of Canada).

Many countries have paid maternity but the rules and conditions of that leave are specific to that country. For instance, in the Czech Republic, a mother may receive 28 weeks of paid leave if they were working 180 days prior to the pregnancy. In Hungary, mothers can receive 24 weeks of paid maternity but they need to let their employer know in writing about the pregnancy. In addition, some countries allow time off work for breastfeeding. For example, in Spain mothers can have an extra hour of break time per day during work, which can be divided into two half hours until the baby is nine months.

Week Thirty-Nine—Date

"My mom's my idol. She's a wonderful mom who left her dreams to raise fourteen children."

Celine Dion, in *Ladies' Home Journal*

When my child first wakes up now...

The pros and cons about my child's sleeping pattern are...

I find I don't have enough time to...

What is your favorite part of staying at home more?

When we want to relax, we...

Tip: Find creative ways to create a new normal if everything does not go exactly as you predicted.

Fact: If any of your children turn out to have a special education need or a disability, please keep in mind everyone can still accomplish great things. John and Greg Rice were the shortest living twins until John's death in 2005. They grew to just two feet ten inches tall. They made their fortunes in real estate in Florida, and they were the owners of a multi-million dollar motivational speaking company called Think Big focused on creative problem-solving (*Guinness World Records*).

Week Forty—Date

"Likely as not, the child you can do the least with will do the most to make you proud."

Mignon McLaughlin, *The Second Neurotic's Notebook*

One of the ways my child communicates with me is...

Now, when I think about getting pregnant again/having another baby, I think...

My partner and I are finding our romantic relationship is...

I feel my body is...

Are you getting enough sleep? Why/why not?

FYI: **Sensorimotor Stage**—According to Jean Piaget, a Swiss psychologist who became famous for his groundbreaking work in child development, the first of four developmental stages is the sensorimotor stage—which is birth through 18 to 24 months. According to his theories, babies learn through their senses and physical exploration during this first stage of cognitive development. Piaget lived from 1896 to 1980.

Bath Play: Water play and bath play are excellent options to help babies learn. Children gather information by doing and observing. If you identify the name of the object as you help your baby play with it, they may learn what it is faster. You can offer a variety of sensory stimulation with waterfall toys, bubbles, rubber ducks, using terry cloth hand scrubbers, and splashing.

Month in Review

Month nine, things should be moving along fine! As you overcome some hurdles, others surface. For me, **month nine** was at the end of the summer but I had the most unexpected thing happen. I got extremely sick. The kind of illness when you can't get to a store, you can't drive anywhere and all you can do is hope you have enough supplies in your house to manage. It was awful because at one point my baby was crying in his crib and I did not have the capacity to comfort him. His father and my family were all out of town. I mention this story because it is really helpful to have a few supplies (typical cold medicines, something for a headache, etc.) on hand for an unplanned bout of the flu or cold, and also to have a backup plan. I wish I had arranged for a friend to take the baby beforehand. I really was in quite a quandary because at that time, I had no one to call. Most of my friends were on vacations and my friends who were in town didn't have kids yet, so I didn't feel like I could impose. I had the real concern of passing on my sickness to my child but luckily my baby did not get sick. After three long miserable days, I felt better.

Tip: If you or your baby does get sick, you may want to try a No Touch Thermometer.

❑ **Recap:** As a knowledgeable parent, what have you achieved for your family? Besides the day-to-day baby care, have you managed to get out of the house? If not, how will you do that? What are your baby's milestones? Is your baby starting to eat new types of food? What hurdles have you overcome and what would you do differently? What is your favorite way to spend time with your child? What do you enjoy watching your baby do the most? How are your child's sibling relationships going? Are you managing to fit in some conversations with adults? How is your house getting cleaned? How is your body doing?

❑ **Mom's Treat of the Month:** It's "me" time. I know, it's a pretty exciting time now that your baby's personality is showing through, and this is such a special time in your life that you don't want to miss a second of it, but life is about balance, and it's very important for you to find a few minutes to focus on you. You can do something during a nap time if you must. What did you pick? Please write it here:

❑ **Principles:** *(1) Sleep may feel optional, but it's an essential part of the human existence so try to get some shut-eye for a balanced life. (2) Think about the things you want to teach your child and align your parenting to role-model your goals. For example, if you would like a polite child, be polite. (3) Make the most of any maternity/paternity allotted to enjoy this special time as a family.*

Does time ever fly! Have you thought about your plans for your baby's birthday? It will be here before you know it! It's time to start **Month Ten.**

CHAPTER TEN

Month Ten

Week Forty-One—Date

"Choose always the way that seems the best, however rough it may be; custom will soon render it easy and agreeable."

Pythagoras, philosopher

Does your child love baths? Any memorable bath stories?

I'm different now because...

Who treats you differently? Explain.

Some of my friends have changed because...

Have you made any decisions on what faith you are going to raise your child, if any?

If you have a partner, are you on the same page with your beliefs?

Creating Your Own Path

A single mom who wants to date:

"In my opinion, it's harder for moms who aren't necessarily going to stay with their spouses or their partner, such as myself, because you have to be able to find your identity and be comfortable being single and being comfortable dating and not getting into a complex about feeling guilty spending time away from your child to pursue relationships with other people. It is a little more divided. I think that's something single mothers struggle with."

Sarah, age 27, in the process of "uncoupling"

A single mom who doesn't want to date:

"Oh my gosh, oh my gosh. I have no desire for any man right now in my life. I don't know if it's motherhood or because of the trauma I went through with her father... It's definitely not something I worry about. I definitely would think that any single mom needs not to worry about that, whether they are divorced or newly single, or whether the baby is with the father—so for me, that's not even in the cards. You have a lot to figure out at that point, so far as that, you're the CEO of your home. Until you figure yourself out in that role, you can't look to do anything else. Right now, I'm doing a lot of great things at home with my daughter and there's so many wonderful things happening, but I'm not completely done figuring out what I'm going to do. It's not a stress or anything like that. I just feel at this point in the game I'm not ready for that."

Angie, age 27

Both dads are successful professionals who plan to be in their children's lives.

Feeling Housebound? Here are a few classic movies to cheer you up!:

- ❀ *The Holiday*—Cameron Diaz, Kate Winslet
- ❀ *Romancing the Stone*—Michael Douglas, Kathleen Turner
- ❀ *Overboard*—Goldie Hawn, Kurt Russell

- *Titanic*—Kate Winslet, Leo DiCaprio (I know counterintuitive—but hey, you're alive!)
- *Rudy*—Inspirational Sports Movie—Sean Astin, Ned Beatty
- *Jungle Book* (2016 version—animated)—Jon Favreau
- *Bridget Jones's Diary*—Renee Zellweger, Hugh Grant
- *E.T. the Extra-Terrestrial*—Henry Thomas, Drew Barrymore
- *Elf*—Will Ferrell, James Caan
- *Stranger than Fiction*—Will Ferrell, Emma Thompson
- *Midnight in Paris*—Owen Wilson, Rachel McAdams
- *Groundhog Day*—Bill Murray, Andie MacDowell
- *How to Lose a Man in Ten Days*—Kate Hudson, Matthew McConaughey
- *Indiana Jones and the Temple of Doom*—Harrison Ford, Kate Capshaw
- *Just Like Heaven*—Reese Witherspoon, Mark Ruffalo
- *The Fugitive*—Harrison Ford, Tommy Lee Jones
- *The Proposal*—Ryan Reynolds, Sandra Bullock
- *Transformers* (the first one)—Shia LaBeouf, Megan Fox
- *Manhattan Murder Mystery*—Diane Keaton, Alan Alda
- *Twins*—Arnold Schwarzenegger, Danny DeVito
- *Spy*—Melissa McCarthy
- *Cinderella Man*—Russell Crowe

Week Forty-Two—Date

"No animal is so inexhaustible as an excited infant."

Amy Leslie, *Amy Leslie at the Fair*

One activity I love doing with my child is...

The most common activity I do with my friends these days is...

"Is this your first baby?"
Edna, Lady in Store

"My first and my last."
Peter (Tom Selleck) in the movie,
Three Men and a Baby

What we used to do more of was...

I find relating to my friends who are just getting pregnant now...

What are you enjoying now that you couldn't do when you were pregnant?

The Gift of Good Health: Give your child the gift of good health. Your child needs exercise. Find ways for your little one to crawl, walk, or run to release their energy. Avoid sugary drinks that cause cavities, and avoid training your little one to crave sugars. If your child never starts on sugary drinks then your little one won't need to stop later. It can take several tries to adjust to a certain food, so if your baby doesn't like a fruit or vegetable right away, try it again. Strive to serve your child food with a wide variety of colors, and try to avoid a plate of beige food which can be a sign they are not getting all their nutrients.

Joke: *My baby is turning one soon, so we returned to the newborn wing at the hospital today to reminisce about the good ol' days.*

Week Forty-Three—Date

"You cannot teach a child to take care of himself unless you let him try and take care of himself. He will make mistakes; and out of these mistakes comes his wisdom."

Henry Ward Beecher, clergyman

The most memorable thing that happened this week was...

Food on the floor is typical of children learning to eat regular food. I'm handling it by...

When it comes to discipline I have concerns about...

I have made a choice to...

Shopping with my child is...

Tip: It turns out that emotional tears have a different composition and chemical makeup than those evoked by eye irritants. One soothes with stress hormones while the other cleanses with a saline solution. Baby tears are no different (*Scientific American Mind*, Torregrossa).

Tennis Moms: Few mothers in history have won a Grand Slam. Kim Clijsters from Belgium won it 18 months after she had a baby and then two more times after that (four times total). Margaret Court from Australia won it seven months after her first child was born. Evonne Goolagong Cawley is the only mother in the Open Era to win Wimbledon. In 2018, American Open Era Grand Slam record holder and first-time mother Serena Williams made her first attempt to beat her record only 10-months after her daughter was born and after going through a challenging delivery. Williams said, "*To all the Moms out there, I was playing for you today*." (*BrainyQuote, Guinness World Records, ESPN*). Williams has also been quoted as saying, "*Tennis is a game, family is forever*."

Week Forty-Four—Date

"Before becoming a mother I had a hundred theories on how to bring up children. Now I have seven children and only one theory; love them especially when they least deserve to be loved."

Kate Samperi, author of *Silken Cords*, in *Mothers*

One thing I love about my baby is...

It's difficult when my child...

I want a sitter or nanny who will...

When I think about how I want to discipline my child, I...

What do you love about having time at home with your baby?

A Baby Can Change You: *"I'm usually shy around a lot of people but I found by having kids this other part of me blossomed. I feel adored and not judged. There is nobody I feel as uninhibited or comfortable around. Motherhood takes us back to that essential person that's inside of us. I feel like it's been [baby's first year] the most accelerated year of growth for us."* Linda, stay-at-home mother of two

Tip: One day I was watching *Oprah,* and Maria Shriver was on that episode, and she told the audience she tells her kids she loves them every single day. I thought this was the most wonderful advice ever. I started doing that with my son as an infant and I continue to do it and I feel like it's one of the best things I've done as a parent.

Joke: *No, I would never drink in front of my child. I merely decant the wine before she goes to bed.*

Month in Review

It's **month ten.** By now, you have probably fully-adjusted to having a baby in your life and identifying as a mom. By now, my baby loved throwing toys out of his crib and thrilled that he knew the object would come back if I gave it to him (object permanence). I had learned to bring more than one of each toy if we were going to a public place so it was easier for children to take turns. I had figured out that if I wanted a few concentrated minutes to myself, I would give my child my full attention for 15 minutes first. My son was growing leaps and bounds. He was chatting away but I could only make out a few words strewn together. He loved jumping up and down on my legs more than anything but he could also walk a few steps on the floor before falling down and trying again. We loved going to the wading pool, and reading lots of baby books. We also liked taking walks at the beach and playing in the sand. As I already revealed, he was a speed crawler. Plus, it was time to start planning his first birthday party soon. I was getting the hang of this 'mother role' and I hope you are, too!

☐ **Recap:** How is your baby changing? Is your baby's face changing from those early days? How are you feeling? Are you overwhelmed with postpartum depression or do you feel happy? Are you feeling balanced? Are you planning ahead? Have you written down what you feel grateful for? Do you sing to your child, or dance with your child? If you are feeling down, try to find the joy in the little moments.

❑ **Mom's Treat of the Month:** If you have not taken the plunge yet to use outside care, maybe try and think of who else might be available to take your child for a few hours. Maybe take this Mom's Treat of the Month to find a treat that's social and that includes someone you love. Write down what you choose here:

❑ **Principles:** *(1) Create the life you want, including the traditions that will serve your family into the future. For example, where you hope to celebrate holidays each year. (2) Your goal may be to be the best mother in the world. Even still, continue with your volleyball team or sports activities, stay connected to coworkers and friends and continue to strive to stay part of the community. (3) If you are separating, make sure to register your child support status. You owe it to your child and yourself to ensure you are protected by the law.*

Yay! You're approaching **Month Eleven!** My favorite month of my baby's first year was this month because his personality really came through! Enjoy!

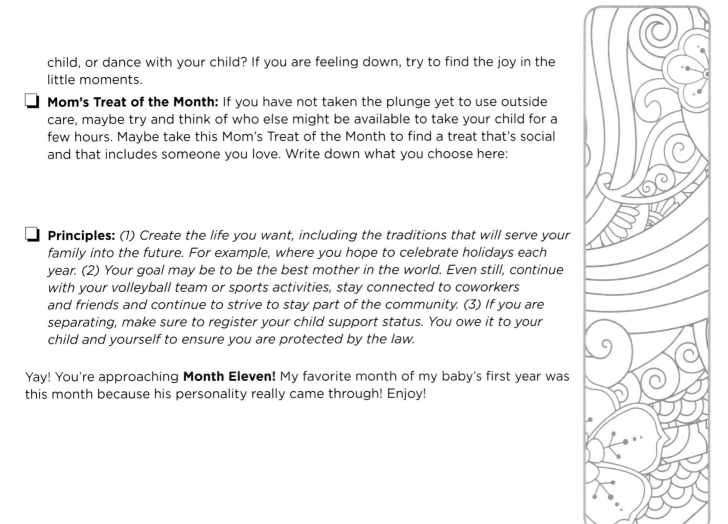

What I want to remember...

CHAPTER ELEVEN

Month Eleven

Week Forty-Five—Date

"Love for children is the enormous untapped power that can wake us to the profound changes we need to make if we're going to have a future worth living."

Raffi, children's singer-lyricist

The most memorable thing that happened this week was...

My partner and I are finding romantic times...

My child loves to...

How many more kids do you wish to have? This week anyway...

I have anxiety when...

"It's real easy to forget what's important, so don't."

Michael Keaton's character Jack in the movie, *Mr. Mom*

Car Safety: Never start the habit of leaving your child in the car. Then you don't have to worry if the temperature is too hot or too cold. Some people don't realize the temperature inside a car doubles and then triples the temperature of the outside air depending on the length of time. By August 2017, there had already been 29 recorded deaths from leaving a child in a hot car. The year ended with a total of 42 child car deaths in the United States (noheatstroke.org).

If the car seat with the baby is too heavy to bring into the house, buy a snap-in car seat and stroller contraption or keep a Radio Flyer® wagon or something similar nearby to roll the baby inside. Clearly, it's better to risk waking up your child than to risk their death. If you are a forgetful person, do not even attempt to do your errands if you're too tired.

Buying in Bulk: Buying and storing extra supplies so you can manage in a pinch is worth it. If when you were single you bought one of each item (paper towels, toilet paper, soap, etc.) maybe consider buying a couple months' supply in advance. It may be time to join a bulk foods store if you're not a member already.

Charger Tip: It can be a lifesaver to have your cell phone charged at all times so you can call for help if you need it. Simplify this process by buying multiple phone chargers so that you have one for the car, your computer, and several of your wall plugs. If you have a charger for your phone in most rooms it won't matter if one of the cords goes missing, which tends to happen eventually. You can also buy a portable charger to keep in your purse.

Tip: For making your purchases easier many people tell me they are turning to the VenMo, PayPal, Apple Pay, Google Wallet or Snapcash.
It might be worth researching!

Joke: *I was born by Cesarean section, but you can't really tell...except when I leave the house, I always go out the window.* Steven Wright, comedian

Week Forty-Six—Date

"Never allow your child to call you by your first name. He hasn't known you long enough."
                                        Fran Lebowitz, *Social Studies*

My favorite babysitter is...

What I find myself worrying about is...

Our sleeping arrangement is...

What have I done lately to participate in cultural events and what's going on in my community? (art show/performance/celebration) (circle)

What have I been happy about this week?

What did my child do that I want to remember?

Childcare Tip: Can't find a sitter? Used up the good graces of relatives? Don't give up. You have Facebook, Meetups, local mommy websites and other forms of social media where you can share your dilemmas with friends and fellow moms and ask for help. Most cities have babysitting and nanny services, such as www.urbansitter. com. Another option is calling your local high school and asking the guidance counselor to suggest potential sitters. Teenagers can take courses to be certified sitters through the Red Cross and other registered organizations. Try talking to other mothers at the park or baby groups for ideas. Organizing a nanny share can create big savings. A nanny share means that you and another family share a nanny who is willing to watch two children at a time or alternate which days he or she works with which family.

Please do your own research before using any service. However, a few babysitting solutions to consider include:

- ❀ Care.com (serves 50 states and 20 countries, including Canada)
- ❀ hellochime.com (for Boston, Chicago, New York City, and Washington, DC)
- ❀ Helpr-app.com (for Los Angeles, Ventura County, Orange County, and San Francisco Bay Area)

Joke: *When is the worst time to tell your husband you're having twins? On the way to the hospital.*

Week Forty-Seven—Date

"We are having our second baby 11 years after our first one. Yes, I'm still with the same dad, we're just bad at family planning."

Helen—married mother of one (soon-to-be two) kids

"We did it backwards, we got married first."

Kara—relating to all her friends who had children before marrying

If someone were to ask how my child is doing, I'd say...

The greatest thing about having a new baby in my life is...

But when I blow-dry my hair and shower, I have to put my child...

I feel grateful for...

What milestones do I remember this week?

Whose company am I enjoying these days?

Keeping the house in order: It can be a real treat to yourself to stay current in this battle to keep things from piling up. I always had a hidden nook reserved for kids stuff, usually the pantry off the kitchen. Once, I had a secret door in the living room where a fireplace used to be. I kept my baby stuff in there and as my baby grew into a toddler he loved having this little spot to hide or find a toy. For some helpful encouraging words try *The Life-Changing Magic of Tidying Up*—Marie Kondo. I use *Clear Your Clutter with Feng Shui*—Karen Kingston. If you prefer television, watch a few episodes of the touching series, *Queer Eye,* available on Netflix. My personal inspiration comes from Goldie Hawn's character in *Overboard* organizing that dumpy house.

Nursery/Finger Rhymes Tip: A nursery rhyme is a poem or song for children that tells a story. If you haven't already, you may want to buy a book of finger rhymes to play with your child. They are mainly nursery rhymes but you learn how to act out the rhymes with your fingers and hands and sometimes your body. One famous example is "I'm a Little Teapot." Others, such as "Once I Caught a Fish Alive" can help little ones learn to count.

Week Forty-Eight—Date

"...love them, feed them, discipline them and let them go free. You will have a lifelong good relationship."

Mary G.L. Davis, *Mothers*

The most memorable thing that happened this week was...

If I ever have another child, one thing I will definitely do differently is...

The best part about working/not working (circle) as a mother is...

Are you accumulating too many things? What would you like to do about it?

What am I doing to learn something this week?

Susanna Moves Closer to Family:

Susanna is a corporate lawyer, with a daughter who is almost two years old. She gave birth to her daughter in Toronto, Canada where she lived for many years and became a partner at her law firm.

After becoming a mother, she realized that she wanted her daughter to have a close relationship with her parents. It mattered so much to Susanna, she was willing to switch law firms and move across the country.

"Talk about a major life change. About six months after she was born, I realized I needed to be near family.

It was less about this is not going to work and more about this is what I want. This is what I want my daughter to grow up with. When she was six months old, we took our first flight to Vancouver, British Columbia to

stay with my mom and dad for a month. My parents came to visit when she was born, again when she was three months old and then I came to see them when she was six months and when she was nine months.

I think the seed was planted when she was six months old. I started to realize how important routine is and I could see the strength of my daughter's relationship with my mom and my dad. I could see the joy she got from them and the joy they got from her. I grew up with my mom's parents in Montreal and my dad's parents in the Okanagan Valley. I saw them quite a bit but not massive amounts, and I realized I didn't want my parents to be holiday parents.

I didn't want them flying in from Vancouver for a month, screwing up our schedule and taking her out of daycare or whatever. I wanted her growing up with my parents as part of her life. Being an older mom, my parents are older grandparents and hitting 70 years old this year. They are very active and very healthy, but shit happens..."

She has a family of me. The most valuable thing I could give her is her family and her history, knowing her grandparents.

It's not a fast decision when you pick up your life and leave your house, your job, your friends and community to move to another place and start over. It's not a quick decision. And you have to take a whole lot of steps backward in some ways. It came down to, I wanted her to have my parents and I want my parents to have her.

I miss Toronto and I miss my friends. You know how it is. It's not so much about the place, it's the relationships you build and having a really strong network. I had that in Toronto but I don't have that in B.C. I haven't been back to Toronto yet, but I think I will. It's hard to travel right now."

Book Recommendation: *Grandma Loves You!* by Helen Foster James, Petra Brown (Illustrator).

Month in Review

Month eleven was heaven. It was my favorite month of my baby's first year. My baby's walking milestone was on the horizon. He was babbling away. I felt like I was starting to know his personality. I could see the world of the toddler around the corner and I felt satisfied I had gotten this far. I had a sense of accomplishment. I still had hurdles to overcome—I had given myself one year to not criticize my physical shape and I was still not all the way back fitness wise. Yet, I was now able to put my baby in a jogging stroller and go. We were still on preschool waiting lists. At the end of the day, I was managing! Who said parenting is impossible? We were in month eleven and both healthy.

I was looking forward to his birthday in another month so I could put together a gathering for friends and family. I was the first parent in my peer group and my friends were being amazing. They had adjusted to my mom status and were helping out more often. My friend Alison and her husband Paul would even borrow my baby for parenting practice. Alison and my baby are both blonds (her hubby and I are brunettes). Alison would tell me how she loved it when people on the street would think she was his mama and ask her about her little one. I assumed my son was well-behaved in their care and they didn't say anything otherwise. On his first birthday, they gave me a card with a picture of their two smiling faces holding up my screaming crying child. Oh my! We had a good laugh. I'm glad they were not deterred by his tantrums! =)

Recap: Looking back on **month eleven,** how are your relationships (romantic, friendships, family)? Are you losing touch with the original you, or are you growing as a person? How can you find your footing if you need to? Who out there can help? Do people treat you differently? How so? Do you want to have more kids? Timeline? If you need more free time, can social media help you find a path to success? How are your baby's sleeping and eating patterns?

☐ **Mom's Treat of the Month: It's month eleven!** By now you've realized this parenting thing isn't going away. You're able to deal with so much stuff! You're an expert on newborns. You've put some thought into your home life, career, and choices. You've thought about family relationships and how you want them to evolve. It is more critical than ever to find that parent versus independent person balance. A sure way to do that is to take a break from your home or work life and carve out a few minutes for yourself. My suggestion for your treat this month is to go out and soak in the world. If you can afford to take a trip, wonderful. If it's local, walk around an area you've never seen before, or visit a neighborhood that makes you happy. Walk into shops, have a bite to eat, visit nature. Remember there's a world out there to explore. Please write your **Mom's Treat of the Month here:**

❏ **Principles:** *You get one shot at living your life. There's no second round, so try to be present, be conscious of your decisions. (1) Analyse the risks and rewards when you make decisions. Make sure you're not taking a risk you couldn't live with. A momentary convenience or desire, it is usually not worth it if there's a chance of an irreversible negative outcome. (2) If you have a big goal, such as moving closer to your parents or buying a house in a more kid friendly suburb, the restructuring and upheaval in the short term might be worth it in order to reap great rewards in the long term.*

This is it, you're onto **Month Twelve!** Your first year of motherhood is almost complete.

CHAPTER TWELVE

Month Twelve

Week Forty-Nine—Date

"Love is always open arms. If you close your arms about love you will find that you are left holding only yourself."
Leo Buscaglia, *Love*

I never anticipated...

My baby talks and says...

My baby can crawl, stand, walk, run, dance (circle)...

My thoughts about breastfeeding are...

My child is sleeping...

I miss a few things from my pre-child days, such as...

Joke: *What do you call a mom on a road trip? A stay-in-the-car mom.*

Tatiana Travels with a Newborn

Tatiana is a married mother of three who lives in New Jersey. Her children are seven and five years old and she has a four-month-old. She says she struggled with a strict schedule with her first child. She says now she is more relaxed. Here is her story of taking her baby on a trip to Los Angeles.

> *"We took Harrison, my youngest, to Los Angeles for a week when he was five weeks old. I would never have been comfortable doing this with the other two. Yet this turned out to be a such an enjoyable week. We took him to all the fun celebrity spots and took pictures of him in front of the iconic LA scenes.*
>
> *Even though I was breastfeeding with my pump and had bottles spread all over the hotel room, we still managed to get out a few nights using a local nanny who was referred to us by a friend. We enjoyed 'Harrison time' during the day and had valuable husband and wife time at night.*
>
> *One of my friends said, 'How did you manage to bring all the newborn gear on the plane with you?' I replied with the fact that he could do without all of his 'gear' for a week. A pack n' play, his stroller, and breast milk were all he really needed. I know that I would have been stressed traveling to LA with my first baby and probably would have opted out. It just shows how much you learn and adjust with the experience of each baby."*

First Year Baby Travels Mini-Checklist

"I find myself having a lot more fun with my kids when I live my life while having them come along for the ride."   Tatiana, New Jersey mother of three

❏ This year we are not going anywhere! Draw your face when you think of this:

❏ We are traveling to see family (who/where/when/to do what):

❏ Vacations we are taking this year:

❏ In the future we want to go to _____ (with/without child) (circle)

Week Fifty—Date

"My opinion is that the future good or bad conduct of a child depends on its mother."
Letizia Ramolino Bonaparte, Napoleon's mother, *Mothers*

The most memorable thing that happened this week was...

"God could not be everywhere so he made mothers." **Proverb**, in *Mothers*

Ways I've learned to distract my child are...

I have had to childproof my house because...

Things are a little better because...

I'm teaching my child to...

The most adult activity I did this week was...

Movie Fact: The little baby in the 1972 movie, The Godfather, is Francis Ford Coppola's real-life daughter Sophia Coppola. She plays the role of Michael Corleone's nephew and godson, Michael Francis Rizzi, being baptized.

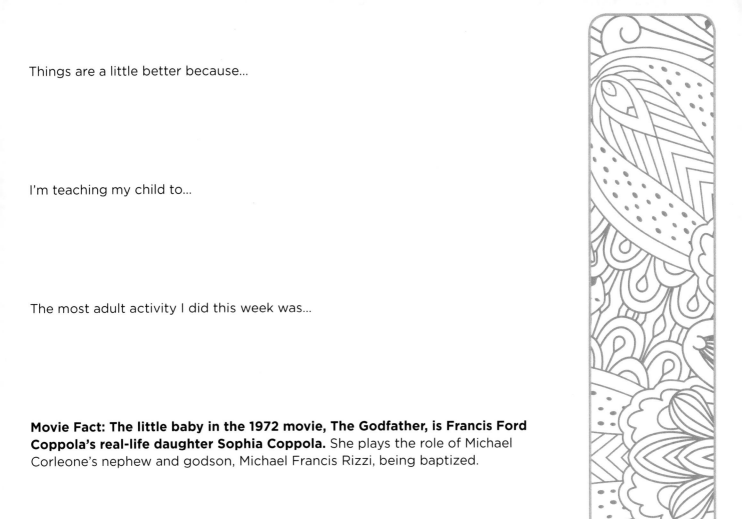

The Godfather became one of the top-grossing movies in history winning Best Picture at the Academy Awards. Coppola also won the award for Best Screenplay (screenplay based on material from another medium) with Mario Puzo and received an Oscar nomination for directing.

Later, in 2004, his daughter, Sophia Coppola won the Oscar for Best Screenplay, (original material) for the movie, *Lost in Translation.* She wrote, directed, and produced the movie which was nominated for Best Picture and she was also nominated for Best Director.

Movie Stats: At a time when 50.8% of the US population is female, only 7.3% of the country's top-grossing 100 films are directed by women. According to the Director's Guild of America, 16% of all films made in 2018 were directed by women. If you want a baby break or family vacation, you may consider hitting up the Sundance Film Festival in Park City, Utah, where 37% of the films were directed by women in 2018. I wonder how many were also mothers, such as Ondi Timoner, who won the Jury Prize twice, both in 2004 and 2009 for her documentaries.

Joke: *Why didn't the baby like loud action movies? He couldn't hear himself cry.*

Week Fifty-One—Date

"Nothing else will make you as happy or sad, as proud or as tired, for nothing is quite as hard as helping a person develop his own individuality especially while you struggle to keep your own."

Marguerite Kelly and Elia Parsons, in *The Mother's Almanac*

What did you do for yourself this week?...

What do you feel about my child turning one?...

For my child's birthday, I'm planning to...

What are you doing for your child's birthday? How is that going?

With all this experience behind you, what do you want to tell new moms?

Moms Tips to New Moms

☐ **Write a letter to your child every year.** You can include information about their life, special gems of knowledge you want to share, or even include descriptions of current world events and how they are being perceived. *"I had a journal the first year of my baby's life and the tip I remember most is that it said to write a letter to your child every year. I have three kids and I have done that. I put them in an envelope and sometimes I include a picture. I write the names of their friends and some advice. My father said the other day that I should give the letters to them now and not wait. The older ones are nine and 11 years old. If I do, I will take a photocopy since they might lose them. I might do it."* Leila, mother of three

☐ **Toys.** Does your living room look like a kids room? You are not a better parent if you can prove the abundance of toys your child has by having them strewn around the house. It is not symbolic of your love, it simply means toys are everywhere. For your sanity (if it bothers you) and health (not tripping as you walk through the house) consider putting most of your baby's toys out of the way. It can result in your child appreciating the toys for longer since they don't see them until they come out again. Toys will seem new all over again. There are easy solutions to help this process, such as putting them in a chest with a lid, in a closet, or by simply reducing the number of toys.

Checklist—Food Tips for a Modern Mom

❑ **Grocery delivery:** If you are still finding it a challenge to eat well with everything going on, see if your city has Instacart for grocery delivery. Search www.instacart.com. Another recommendation is Amazon Fresh.

❑ **Farm fresh vegetables delivered or for pick up:** I have tried having organic vegetables delivered which is amazing. Try picking up a Farm Fresh delivery service in your area which brings farm-fresh vegetables to your house. Another option is ordering groceries in advance and picking them up at the store, Whole Foods offers this service.

❑ **Meals ready to cook:** You can also try ordering a delivery program, such as Fresh Prep. They provide all the ingredients ready-to-make, so all you need to do is cook them up!

❑ **Try an Instant Pot**®**:** If you're one of those moms who like to cook for your family, you might want to try an Instant Pot 7-in-1 electric pressure cooker. They save time and you can make delicious meals, whether a novice chef or a connoisseur.`

Week Fifty-Two—Date

"A mother's love is reflected in the joyful faces of her loved ones."
Anonymous

The most memorable thing that happened to me this week was...

When my child is around dogs and cats...

I like/don't like (circle) to have my child around animals because...

When I reflect on the past year, I...

Other than myself, my child spends the most time with...

Name your pets and how they are getting along with your baby...

"The more that you read, the more things you will know. The more you learn, the more places you'll go."

Dr. Seuss, *I Can Read With My Eyes Shut*

Book Tip: In my opinion, the first year is not complete without sharing at least one of Dr. Seuss' books, such as *Oh, the Places You'll Go!* If you are ever feeling down and need a pick-me-up this book might be just what you need and your little one will enjoy being read to as well.

Reading to Infants: It's common to wait to read to babies until they are almost two years old; however, it is never too soon to start. Children learn all the sounds they need to know in order to learn their native language in the first year. Reading can help with communication skills, learning about the world, memory building, and exposure to more words. It can even strengthen the bond between you and your child. There are a lot of wonderful kids books. Hard books are an excellent option if your child is teething or might be tempted to rip pages (Center for Early Literacy).

Year in Review

Congratulations! **Month twelve.** Your baby is officially a year old. You can look back at the past twelve months and think about all that you have accomplished. You may have uncovered some of the magical mysteries of motherhood and learned how big your heart grew by having this new child in your life.

Short story: As you think about celebrating this momentous first birthday it's a good time to reflect on the friends and family in your baby's life. It's wonderful to give your child the gift of casting a wide social net. I always tried to include as many people who wanted to be in my son's life as possible. My goal was that if anything ever happened to me, he would have other people he cared about and who cared about him.

While I was in full-time university with my son from the time he was six weeks old to five months old, I was approached by two first-year university students, Alison and Luke, who I had never met before. They approached me because they wanted the opportunity to spend time with my son. After I found out it would be safe, I agreed to let them. They would take my son and hang out on the steps of the university building separately from me (within my eye view). I would joke with my classmates *"He has his own friends"*—he was two months old. They never asked for money to babysit. They just enjoyed his company. Incidentally, that couple got married and now have two children of their own.

❏ **Recap:** What milestones has your baby reached this year? Is your baby walking? Talking? Who are your baby's friends? Who are your friends? What do you feel you have accomplished? Have you managed to travel or have you mainly nested at home? What hurdle have you overcome that you are proud of? Have you started reading to your child? Have you thought about the wisdom you hope to impart on your child in the future?

❑ **Mom's Treat of the Month:** As much as this book has advocated the importance of finding time for yourself and for balance in this overwhelming first year of motherhood, let's face it—it's a lot easier said than done. I was with my baby almost 24/7 that first year. If you are one of those moms, please take some time this weekend to yourself. If you are one of those moms who powered back into your career full-force and feel saddened that you did not get to spend as much time as you wanted with your child, then your Mom's Treat of the Month is the opposite. Plan a special day to spend with your child, take some pictures and treasure that you brought this little being into your life. If you had perfect balance, well lucky you! That calls for a date night! ;)

❑ **Principles:** *(1) You are human! Doing your best is the most anyone can expect. (2) Be proud that you are raising a member of the human race and you are contributing. It is a lot of work to raise a baby, whether you have support or not. It's a huge undertaking. (3) Life is better if you can feel grateful.*

You did it! Pat yourself on the back. You have accomplished one year of motherhood! You have graduated to the mother of a toddler.

AC: After Child's First Year

"A dog's love is only second to that of a mother's."

Radhika Mundra, *Goodreads*

How does it feel to have reached the one year milestone?

Looking back on the year, what was the biggest highlight?

What are you looking forward to in year two?

What do you hope to teach your child next year?

What's your personal resolution for the next phase?

Bad Mom Movies: Wondering if you did a good job this year? Watch these and if see yourself acting like this in the future, maybe not! ;)

- *I, Tonya*—Margot Robbie, Allison Janney
- *Lady Bird*—Greta Gerwig, Laurie Metcalf
- *Home Alone*—Macaulay Culkin, Catherine O'Hara
- *Cinderella*—Many to choose from!

Movie-Pick-Me-Up: I can watch *Kevin Hart: I'm a Grown Little Man* (stand up comedy) over and over. It's hilarious and he talks about parenting with his new baby. If you want to feel empowered nothing beats a little *Wonder Woman* starring Gal Gadot and Chris Pine.

Game-Pick-Me-Up: Feeling social? Gather up a few people and try the interactive game Fibbage™: The Hilarious Bluffing Game by Jackbox Games™. You might be surprised how fast your dilemmas du jour drift away for a few minutes. Another fun game with a small group is GeoWhere Geography™. It's an app that shows you a location and you have to guess where in the world it is.

What I want to remember...

CHAPTER THIRTEEN

Overcoming Adversity

"Tears never bring anything back. Life is a struggle and a good spy gets in there and fights."

Ole' Golly's character in Louise Fitzhugh, *Harriet the Spy*

Every mother copes with problems, whether it is a medical issue, a move, or a difficult relative. There is always something. In my case, I happened to be in a full-time university program where I knew no one, without a budget for babysitters, and during the dead of winter. Here are a few stories of mothers who had to cope with adversity during the first year of their baby's life and how they managed.

The Car Accident

Amanda is a married mother of four children who lives in Vancouver, British Columbia. She managed to raise her first three daughters primarily on her own while working as a director of communications. Amanda loved her job, she was a passionate employee who appreciated the independence her career gave her. Her daughters were born when she was 22, 24, 26, and 41 years old.

After her divorce during her late 30s, Amanda fell in love with a man who didn't have any children of his own. They married, and Amanda became pregnant with her fourth child. She planned to continue her chosen profession.

Then, life took an unexpected turn. Driving in the middle of a typical day, a car smashed into the back of Amanda's vehicle. At seven months pregnant, her life changed forever. The driver behind her had a schizophrenic episode. Unable to pass Amanda in a congested traffic lane, he convinced himself he could push her out of the way and barreled into her car in full force. This is her story:

238

"For me, the difference with this child was that I stopped working. I didn't plan on it and it's been a huge adjustment because I loved my job."

Unable to work, Amanda started relying more on her husband than she had in the past.

"I had to let go of that control. It was me and the three girls for so long, and I'm so used to being independent. Not only was I letting go of my independence by not having a job, but I was being to be dependent on someone else and having another person depend on me. I still struggle with that.

I really feel like with the fourth baby I lost my independence, which I worked very hard to maintain since I worked very hard at being a single mother."

She says her body was in a different state due to being pregnant. She had concussions, anxiety, and post-traumatic stress. She now has anxiety over her other kids driving. She also had severe tissue damage that makes it hard for her to hold her baby and short-term memory damage from the concussions, making it impossible for her to work.

"I had been holding the steering wheel, so when she was born I could barely pick her up. There was so much soft tissue damage to my arm. To make matters worse, the seat belt damaged my milk ducts. I didn't know if she wasn't getting milk. I didn't know at first that I was starving my baby."

They tried to supplement with formula and a drug that was supposed to let down her milk, but there was too much damage to the milk ducts. She says it was heartbreaking.

She was still employed when the car accident occurred. Although she was aware she would be taking a break to go on maternity, it never occurred to her that she wouldn't be going back.

> *"I wasn't physically capable of returning to work. More importantly, I had short-term memory problems from the concussions. I have had so many challenges, plus I had the other three girls and dealing with them."*

Amanda says she will never really be the same. Her husband has been wonderful driving the older kids to all their activities and competitive sports games. They bought a house in Italy where she goes for two months in the summer with her youngest baby. She credits Pilates as her saving grace. She says it eases the pain of her injuries and she meets interesting women she would normally not encounter. They talk before class and after. Unfortunately, Amanda was not able to have more children, which was devastating for her and her husband who were looking forward to creating a bigger family. She finally came to the realization that the next baby in her life will be a grandchild. She is grateful for what she has.

The Full-Term Miscarriage: Finding the strength to become a mother after losing a previous baby full-term.

Samantha is a 28-year-old stay-at-home mom. Her husband is in the Canadian Navy and he came home for a 10-month paternity leave. They live in Lower Sackville, Nova Scotia. She has a three-year-old daughter and a four-month-old son. Between the two, she had a full-term miscarriage and lost a son. She explains how parenting is different this time around.

Living with fear

"I worry about my new baby dying and about things that I can't really control. With my daughter, she's my first and 'it's out there' [meaning death] and I took safety precautions, but I didn't really think anything bad would happen.

But when I lost my son after a full-term pregnancy, I began worry about SIDS. I didn't realize it would be such a challenge worrying about my new baby boy. I'm getting a little better as he gets older. It wasn't postpartum depression, it didn't feel like that. I felt a fear that this can happen since it's happened to me before."

Learning to cope

"I go to the gym every day. And that's really important to me mentally to work out so I can get that grief and anxiety out. I never really left my daughter. Instead, I took her for walks with me. I do leave my son with my husband which is something I never did with my daughter. He's off until April and my son will be nine months.

After I lost my first son, I knew that if anything ever happened again, I would never try again. My husband had a vasectomy and that makes

him really happy because he knows we never have to go through that again. He already booked it before I even had my third baby.

I had my [second] son early. I was induced at 36 weeks because the doctors didn't want my delivery to go over the date that I lost my [first] son. So it was all planned and I had to go in a month early. They actually had the same due date, a day apart. I found out on the same day that they were a year apart from each other and that they were both boys. It wasn't planned out like that."

The emotional challenge of moving on

"It was hard because we had a name picked out right away for the son that I lost. His name was George and he was born on the same day as the prince, and everybody at the hospital was going on about his name.

When it happened, I said that I would never have any more kids. I was done, but as time went on, I really wanted to give Molly a sibling. Even though she was young, she understood, so I really wanted to try again because I didn't feel like I was done with my life until I had one more child. But no, at the start, I didn't want to try again right away.

I made sure to talk to people, to make sure people know what happened. I didn't want people to think something had been wrong with him. I talked about him a lot. You know, he was my child. Even though he didn't live, he was still a full-term eight pounds, he was a baby. I talked about him a lot, cried when I needed to, and exercised. I'm not fully through it, but that's how I get through it."

Losing her dad shortly after

"I lost my dad seven months later when I was pregnant with Rupert. We named my son's middle name after my father, Terence. My dad was the most supportive person when my baby died. My father said one thing that made me decide I wanted to try again.

My dad said, 'It's only nine months of your whole life.'"

Your instincts and feeling helpless

"I remember everything. A lot of people didn't believe me because I said I didn't feel well and I begged the doctors not to send me home. I was only 38 weeks so I was two weeks early. They were saying my uterus wasn't fully ready, to just go home and rest, and we'll try again. I wasn't fully dilated. I was around four cm,. but his head wouldn't engage because I had too much water. I just knew there was something wrong, but they sent me home. I knew he wasn't moving as much.

I remember the night he died (obviously I didn't know for sure until the autopsy) but I remember when I stopped feeling him move. I just remember crying in my bed that night and crying to my husband

because I had an overwhelming feeling that I was going to die in childbirth.

And my husband said, 'You gotta stop thinking like that.' I would explain that I just felt something was going to go wrong and I'm going to die or whatever. He said, 'You need to calm down.' And that was the night before. I thought I was dying, but it was really him.

The next morning I woke up and I realized I hadn't felt him move since the night before, and then I went through the day and I didn't feel him move. Someone said to me, 'Stop worrying, he's just tired. Nobody really believed me. I went in the next morning and told them to check for his heartbeat and they did and he didn't have a heartbeat.

The birth of my next boy was entirely different. I did it naturally. My water broke, his head was already engaged and it was a really easy delivery. I just stayed a day later because he had a little jaundice. I have slept really well since I had him, but for the first little while, I would worry about SIDS and touch him a lot, maybe a little too much, but then I got that Angelcare® monitor [it's not recommended to have those at home], and I know it doesn't prevent it but it helps a lot. It helps me just hearing that noise. I have actually had a good sleep from the start. He goes to bed with me at seven, and I'll read and he'll be asleep, and then he'll get up every three hours and nurse.

I thought my daughter was easy but she nursed every two hours around the clock. I didn't mind because she was my first and I didn't know any different and I didn't care.

Rupert will nurse all the time during the day but I don't mind. I kind of offer it. At night he goes three hours and that is like heaven because my daughter was feeding so much more, and it seems so easy with him. I don't have any complaints (laughs), I sleep fine with him."

How they deal as a couple

"My husband and I have been married four years, and been together for five years. Three babies in four years is a lot. He relaxes by playing online video games with my brothers and his friends from work. He walks our dog; we have a chocolate lab.

I have so much weight lifted off me now that I'm done and that I have my children and I'm so young. It's kind of sad knowing that you're never going to have more kids but I know I don't want to have anymore.

I worry because they never really found out why he died. The autopsy came back that he was healthy and normal and nothing was wrong with me, so I still don't know what happened exactly. My getting pregnant again and not knowing that was going to happen was really stressful because I was high risk. I had ultrasounds all the time from 28 weeks on. I had every test that you could think of and I was monitored closely even though that wouldn't have changed anything if it was to happen again. It was basically like I was on red alert for nine months of my life, and when my dad died during my pregnancy that made it even worse.

My dad knew that I was having a boy and at least he got to see me pregnant and I got to tell him I was going to name my next baby after him."

A mother knows her baby even while it's in the womb

"With George, we had his name picked out. I feel like I got to connect to him a little more. A lot of people think because your baby died inside you, they brush it off like a miscarriage, they don't think it's as serious. I feel like I was the only person who really knew George so that was hard because I had time with him.

George's pregnancy was so different from Molly and Rupert. I always sensed something was wrong. I didn't feel right. I always felt like I was never really going to meet him.

I had a [medically] healthy pregnancy with George (no throwing up or anything) but I had a lot of anxiety. I don't talk about it because it makes me sound crazy, but I had an irrational fear that someone was going to steal my daughter from me. I know all moms worry about that, but it was so severe when I was pregnant with George. And my husband would say, 'That's not going to happen.' But I had an overwhelming feeling and after George died it went away. I didn't have that feeling anymore, after the pregnancy and after George died.

I had this feeling someone was going to take my child from me and I couldn't do anything about it. I thought that it was Molly because George was inside me, I felt what it would be like for someone to *steal my child. I don't feel like that anymore. It's no because I lost my child, because I don't sense that with my daughter and I don't sense that with Rupert. It was just when I was pregnant with George. It was overwhelming."*

Samantha's experience has left her feeling the need to advocate for mothers about the importance of intuition. She believes she should not have been sent home from the hospital that day, and hopes that other mothers will be brave and stand their ground with doctors when they're feeling particularly vulnerable about their pregnancies. Samantha is part of a big family, she has five siblings including her fraternal twin. She continues to hold dear to family values and is grateful for her husband and two healthy children as they move forward together.

Note: The American Academy of Pediatrics (AAP) states cardiorespiratory devices should not be used as a strategy to reduce SIDS. AAP provides a list of recommendations of what parents should do on their website www.aap.org. SIDS is described as infant deaths that cannot be explained after significant analysis. Parents who do use baby monitors must be careful not to rely on them and still keep careful tabs themselves. If you do want to use a baby monitor, here are a few varieties:

- Infant Optics DXR-8 Video Baby Monitor® with Interchangeable Optical Lens at www.infantopticsdxr8.org.
- The Snuza® Hero SE Baby Movement Monitor can let parents know if their baby is breathing, available at www.snuza.com.
- Owlet® focuses on your baby's heart rate and oxygen levels. Smart Sock 2®
- Angelcare® monitors (Angelcare AC517®) at www.angelcarebaby.com.
- Baby Movement Monitor with 5" Touchscreen Display and Wireless Sensor Pad®

When Dad is Deployed

Kara is 27 years old and a first-time mother. Her husband, who just turned 30, is in the United States Marine Corps. They recently bought a house in North Carolina. Her husband is on duty about 50 percent of the time and is currently deployed at the time of the interview. Kara says that when he's deployed their communication is extremely limited and she receives only a handful of phone calls throughout his whole deployment. They can only communicate by email. Although her husband hasn't seen their daughter since she was a newborn—a long seven and a half months ago—they will be reunited soon.

Returning home

"My husband is in the military so we have been sort of shuffled around. He was deployed when our daughter was two months old, so we [Kara and her newborn] drove from San Diego to Massachusetts where I have family. Then, we drove from Massachusetts down to Florida. Then, I bought a house in North Carolina, so it's been absolutely insane.

My husband's coming home in five days. I'm in the freak out stage. I'm looking at pictures when she was a newborn. I mean she wasn't even holding her head up and now she's basically a toddler [nine and half months old], it's insane.

We were married for about three years before being pregnant. We just wanted to enjoy being married, you know. We were kind of backward, I mean all of my friends back home have kids but are single, so I grew up in an environment where everybody was having kids and not getting married."

Road trips with a newborn

"I had just bought a Jeep Patriot and I had my dog, too—she's my first child. I call her my fur child. My daughter's Godmother ended up flying out from Milwaukee and we did the first leg together. Then I drove by myself to Ohio where my grandfather is, and then I drove from Ohio to Massachusetts, with some stops on the way.

Driving isn't that big for me, but having a baby was definitely different. Unfortunately, because of the trauma of how she was brought into the world, my body wouldn't produce milk. I think I got six ounces one time and that was it.

I was 41 weeks when I went in to get induced. I was in labor for 26 hours and the last six hours I was just pushing consecutively with every contraction. They failed to check to see if she was a breach or not, so by the time they did I was so swollen. I wish I had done a natural birth. I was 10 cm dilating so maybe I could have done it but I feel like they dropped the ball—so we had to get an emergency C-section—because the doctor came in and he was freaked out because he doesn't usually let patients push more than three hours. He was scared for me. He was worried about her blood pressure dropping. So we just went in and had a C-section and that's how she was born.

I tried breastfeeding. They put this little tube on me to supplement breastfeeding, so she was still at the breast, but it was really hard. I did a lot of research about breastfeeding. I didn't think of formula, but it was a major surgery and I was not really able to move, so after hearing my daughter cry, I couldn't do anything except for having someone bring my daughter a bottle.

My husband was there for her birth. Then he had to leave for two weeks, come home for two weeks, and then leave for two more weeks of training. After that, he was deployed for the next 217 days.

Her birth is a big thing. My friend, Angie and I talked about our birth plans, We had it down to exactly how it's going to go and there was no birth plan. I know our stories are different but they definitely did not go the way we were talking about them when we were pregnant at prenatal yoga.

The breastfeeding is the bond I never got to have with her. I'd cry sometimes, but I've gotten over it. It's not as sad as when I couldn't do anything for her. I keep her on track with her bottles because I feel bad that I wasn't able to do that for her.

I realize, now that I have a formula baby, that I'm hated. I understand the ones that are so vain they are like, 'Oh no, I'm not going to have my kid at my boob.' But it's like, 'No, I tried!' So I'm part of this taboo group of people. Angie is so supportive, so I don't get that from her, but formula fed moms is a crazy term to me because how do you know what people's struggles are?

My husband hasn't really been able to spend time with the baby either. Everyone's like your husband's going to come home and are you going to have a deployment baby. I say, 'No, I started birth control months ago.' We haven't been a family. I feel so bad for him. I'm excited for him to come home. He finally got orders for North Carolina, so we are going home to all be together.

It's so funny—when everybody asks me if I'm going to have more kids, especially because I'm married. It depends on the day of the week (laughs). Some days I would love to have a couple more and I talk about if I have another baby what I'm going to do next time. Then there are other days when I'm like, 'No, I'm absolutely blessed and why mess with perfection?' (laughs)"

Reflecting on the First Year: What has been your biggest challenge to overcome or what circumstance would you like to reflect on during this first year of motherhood? Write your story here:

More space to write...

Mommy Milestones and Charts

Baby Trips Chart

Date	Trip Location	How It Went

There's a First Time for Everything

The First Time	Date	How It Went
The first time my baby rode in the car		
The first time baby came home from the hospital		
The first time I went out with the baby		
The first time I went out without the baby		
The first time I went on a date without the baby		

The First Time	Date	How It Went
The first time I managed to get a haircut as a mother		
The first time I had a manicure and/or pedicure		
The first time I drove around to put the baby to sleep		
The first time I did something creative to put the baby to bed		
The first time I wore clothes I could wear before I had a baby		

The First Time	Date	How It Went
The first time the baby slept through the night		
The first time I noticed I'm wearing "mom" clothes		
The first time I had to remind myself I might wanna brush my teeth, shower, comb my hair or wear clothes without stains before heading out		
The first time with a sick baby		
The first argument I had over child-rearing		

The First Time	Date	How It Went
The first time the baby slept in a bassinet/cradle/my bed		
The first time the baby slept in a crib		
The first time my brain truly seemed to have recovered from pregnancy fog		
The first time having romance again		
The first time giving the baby a bottle		

The First Time	Date	How It Went
The first time I gave myself a bottle after having a baby (of beer, wine, champagne, specialty drink) (circle)		
The first time doing an amazing feat of parental coordination		
First time seeing the baby with real tears		
First time seeing myself with real tears over parenting		
First time my baby had a boo-boo, was hit on the head, or a fall (circle)		

The First Time	Date	How It Went
First time taking the baby on a plane		
First time feeding the baby solid food		
First visible tooth		
First time giving the baby Tylenol® or similar		
First time I had a babysitter		
First time I had a "real" babysitter (not family or friends)		

The First Time	Date	How It Went
First time the baby crawled		
First time TV seemed like a good idea		
First time the baby stood up		
First time the baby slept through the night		
First time the baby took a step		
First time the baby took a few steps		

The First Time	Date	How It Went
First time baby walked		
First baby immunization		
The first clear word my baby said		
The first phrase my baby said		
The first time I stayed out a little longer than I should have for whoever was watching my baby		

The First Time	Date	How It Went
First time...		

The First Time	Date	How It Went

Author's Note: One thing I have learned from my child is that it's advantageous to make life easier. Somehow I got it stuck in my head that life is best when it is a challenge. Although it's great to take on a personal challenge, such as an outdoor adventure or to learn a new skill, it turns out that reducing day-to-day struggles can really lead to a happier more peaceful existence. This book will give you pieces of insight and nuggets of wisdom that will help you solve some of those problems of the day that you are experiencing. May it help you reach your own goals to be the best parent you can be and the best person you can be. Congratulations on the milestone of the first year! I hope you will be back to read *Mom's Turn 2* or on a bad day, *Why Can't I Scream at the Mall?: A Journal for Parenting a Toddler and Stories for Staying Empowered.* Until next time...

Disclaimer: I am not a medical professional and I am not offering any medical advice. This book is not intended as a substitute for the medical advice of physicians. The reader should regularly consult a physician in matters relating to their health or the baby's health, particularly with respect to any symptoms that may require diagnosis or medical attention. Some names and identifying details have been changed to protect the privacy of certain individuals who requested anonymity. All of the advice in this book is merely a guide and all of it should be followed up with your own personal due diligence. The author cannot be held responsible for any individual's parenting choices or health decisions, and the contents of this book are simply a melting pot of ideas. The book contains a wide variety of perspectives, and not all opinions are necessarily shared by the author.

BIBLIOGRAPHY

Chapter One

American Academy of Pediatrics. "Breastfeeding and the Use of Human Milk. March. 2012. Accessed June 2018, http://pediatrics.aappublications.org/content/129/3/e827.

Blake, William. (partial poem) "Infant Joy." Chicago: NTC Contemporary Publishing Group, 1998.

Blake, William. (partial poem) "Infant Sorrow." Chicago: NTC Contemporary Publishing Group, 1998.

Centers for Disease Control and Prevention. National Center for Vital Statistics. "12 Month-ending Age-specific Birth Rates: United States 2015-Quarter 4, 2017." Accessed June 2018, https://www.cdc.gov/nchs/nvss/vsrr/natality-dashboard.htm#.

Centers for Disease Control and Prevention. "Preterm Birth." Reproductive Health. Accessed October 2017, https://www.cdc.gov/reproductivehealth/maternalinfanthealth/pretermbirth.htm.

Central Intelligence Agency Report: "Mother's Mean Age at First Birth." Accessed October 2017, https://www.cia.gov/library/publications/the-world-factbook/fields/2256.html.

Dennis, Cindy-Lee, Ellen Hodnett, Ruth Gallop, Beverley Chalmers. "The Effect of Peer Support on Breast-Feeding Duration Among Primiparous Women: A Randomized Controlled Trial." CMAJ. January 8, 2002. Accessed June 2018, http://www.cmaj.ca/content/166/1/21.short.

Derricotte, Toi. *Natural Birth.* Trumansburg, NY: Crossing Press, 1983.

Drabble, Margaret. *Children—A Brief History of My Addiction.* London: Warren Editions, 1974. Chosen by Alexandra Towle. *Mothers: A Celebration in Prose, Poetry, and Photographs of Mothers and Motherhood.* Riverside, NJ: Simon and Schuster, 1988.

Everts, Sarah. "Alcohol-free Beer May Boost Breast Milk Supply But Still Tastes Good, and a New Enzyme Strips Brews of Buttery Notes." c&en. Accessed June 2018, https://cen.acs.org/articles/94/i11/Alcohol-free-beer-boost-breast. htmlngieering News. Vol. 94, Issue 11. March 14, 2016.

Hamer, Dean H. and Peter Copeland. *Living With Our Genes*. New York, NY: Doubleday, 1998.

Hay, Louise L. *You Can Heal Your Life*. New York, NY: Hay House, 1984.

Jordan, Jennifer. "Cav's Guard J.R. Smith's Social Media Posts Spark Discussion About Premature Births." Fox 8 Cleveland. January 16, 2017. Accessed October 2017, http://fox8.com/2017/01/16/cavs-guard-j-r-smiths-social-media-posts-spark-discussion-about-premature-birth/.

Kingsolver, Barbara. *The Bean Trees*. New York, NY: Harper Perennial, 1998.

Lamott, Anne. *Operating Instructions: A Journal of My Son's First Year*. New York, NY: Anchor Books, 1993.

Lara, Adair. *Welcome to Earth, Mom*. San Francisco, CA: Chronicle Books, 1992.

Lin, Chien-Heng, Hsiu-Chuan Yang, Chien-Sheng Cheng, and Chin-En Yen. "Effects of Infant Massage on Jaundiced Neonates Undergoing Phototherapy." *Italian Journal of Pediatrics*. November 25, 2015. Accessed May 2018, https://www.ncbi.nlm.nih.gov/pmc/articles/PMC4659198/.

March of Dimes. "Premature Babies." Updated October 2013, http://www.marchofdimes.org/complications/premature-babies.aspx#.

Meyers, Nancy, and Charles Shyer. *Baby Boom*. Film. Directed by Charles Shyer. United Artists. 1987.

Perske, Joern, *The Nation*. "Europe's Youngest Premature Baby Turns Five." Article November 17, 2015. Accessed October 2017, http://www.nationmultimedia.com/life/Frieda-the-miracle-girl-30273056.html.

Statistics Canada: "Health Facts Sheets: Preterm Live Births in Canada, 2000 to 2013." October 26, 2016. Accessed May 2018, https://www.statcan.gc.ca/pub/82-625-x/2016001/article/14675-eng.htm.

Statistics Canada. "Report on the Demographic Situation in Canada, 2008 to 2012." Updated July 9, 2013. Accessed August 24, 2017, http://www.statcan.gc.ca/daily-quotidien/130709/dq130709a-eng.htm.

World Health Organization, "10 Facts on Breastfeeding." Updated August 2017, http://www.who.int/features/factfiles/breastfeeding/en/.

Young, Mark C. *The Guinness World Records* [Revised Edition: May 11, 1999]. New York, NY: Bantam, 1999.

Young, Mark C. *Guinness World Records.* Vancouver, BC: Jim Pattison Group, 2017.

Chapter Two

BBC Homepage, "Skeleton—Bone growth." *Science: Human Body & Mind,* September 24, 2014. Accessed September 2017, http://www.bbc.co.uk/science/humanbody/body/factfiles/bonegrowth/femur.shtml.

Cavandish, Marshall. "Skeletal System" in *Mammal Anatomy: An Illustrated Guide.* Tarrytown, NY: 2010. Accessed October 2017, https://books.google.ca/books?id=mTPI_d9fyLAC&pg=PA129#v=onepage&q&f=false.

Hunt, Helen. "All the parents I know are doing impossible tasks every moment," on Showbiz Today, *Ladies' Home Journal.* Iowa: Meredith Corporation, 1998.

Kerr, Jean."Now the thing about having a baby—and I can't be the first person to have noticed this—is that thereafter you have it," in *Please Don't Eat the Daisies.* Garden City, NY: Doubleday, 1957.

Plantiga, Judy and Laurel J. Trainor. "Melody Recognition by Two-Month-Old Infants." 2009. *The Journal of the Acoustical Society of America. 12, EL58.* Accessed June 2018, https://asa.scitation.org/doi/abs/10.1121/1.3049583.

Richardson, Henry H. *Ultima Thule.* In Noda, Hisashi. "A Note on Henry Handel RIchardson." Accessed June 2018, https://core.ac.uk/download/pdf/147424083.pdf.

Seinfeld, Jerry, in Alexandra Towle's *Mothers: A Celebration in Prose, Poetry, and Photographs of Mothers and Motherhood.* Riverside, NJ: Simon and Schuster, 1988.

World Health Organization. "10 Facts on Breastfeeding." Updated August 2017, http://www.who.int/features/factfiles/breastfeeding/en/.

Young, Mark C. *Guinness World Records.* Vancouver, BC: Jim Pattison Group, 2017.

Chapter Three

American Pregnancy Association. "Hair Loss During Pregnancy: Telogen Effluvium." Accessed June 2018, http://americanpregnancy.org/pregnancy-health/hair-loss-during-pregnancy/.

Barr, Ronald G., "What is Colic?" The Period of Purple Crying. Accessed June 2018, http://purplecrying.info/sub-pages/crying/what-is-colic.php.

Bologna, Caroline. "Jimmy Kimmel Says Bill Murray's Parenting Advice is 'Right On!'" October 22, 2014. Updated December 6, 2017, https://www.huffingtonpost.com/2014/10/22/bill-murrays-parenting-advice_n_6029452.html.

Benson, J.G., and J.L. Forman and E.C. Larson, et al. "Mother's Menopause May Predict Daughter's Fertility, Egg Count." November 6, 2012, based on research published in the *Journal of Reproduction.* Accessed November 2017, https://academic.oup.com/humrep/article/28/1/247/595592.

Carson, Lillian. *The Essential Grandparent: A Guide to Making a Difference.* Deerfield Beach, FL, Health Communications Inc., 1997.

Fairbanks, Evelyn. "My children were a constant joy to me, except on days when they weren't" in *The Days of Rondo.* St Paul, MN: Minnesota Historical Society Press, 1990.

Jackson, Marni. "Home alone with a wakeful newborn, I could shower so quickly that the mirror didn't fog and the backs of my knees stayed dry," in *The Mother Zone*. New York, NY: Modern Family Vintage Books, 1992.

Library of Congress. "Today in History—May." Accessed June 2018, https://www.loc.gov/item/today-in-history/may-09#celebrating-mothers.

Peralta, Katherine. "Remarriage on the Rise in the US." November 14, 2014. U.S. News based on a Pew Research Center Report. Accessed October 2017, http://www.pewsocialtrends.org/2014/11/14/four-in-ten-couples-are-saying-i-do-again/.

Science Daily. "Mothers' Age at Menopause May Predict a Daughter's Ovarian Reserve." November 6, 2012. Sourced from European Society of Human Reproduction and Embryology (ESHRE). Accessed January 2018, https://www.sciencedaily.com/releases/2012/11/121106191734.htm.

Virgil (4.60–63). *"Begin, little boy, to recognize your mother with a smile."*

Wolf, Maura. "What are the Benefits of Peppermint Candy?" October 2017. Accessed June 2019, https://www.livestrong.com/article/286699-what-are-the-benefits-of-peppermint-candy/.

Chapter Four

Bureau of Labor Statistics, April 2017. "Women in the Labor Force: A Databook." Accessed June 2018. https://www.bls.gov/opub/reports/womens-databook/2016/home.htm.

Cohn, D'Avera and Andrea Caumont. Pew Research Center. "7 Key Findings About Stay-at-Home Moms." April 2014. Accessed June 2018, http://www.pewresearch.org/fact-tank/2014/04/08/7-key-findings-about-stay-at-home-moms/.

Diller, Phyllis. Brainy Quotes. Accessed March 2018, https://www.brainyquote.com/quotes/phyllis_diller_121653.

Eydal, Gudny Bjork, and Stefan Olafsson. "Demographic Trends in Iceland: First report for the project Welfare Policy and Employment in the Context of Family Change May 2003." Accessed June 2018, http://1ehukb3kd764oddub3rdo4uw-wpengine.netdna-ssl.com/wp-content/uploads/2016/04/icelanddemo.pdf.

Iceland Monitor. "Iceland Leads in Out-of-Wedlock Babies." June 12, 2015. Updated May 9, 2016. Accessed August 2017, https://icelandmonitor.mbl.is/news/politics_and_society/2015/06/12/iceland_leads_in_out_of_wedlock_babies/.

Lazarre, Jane. *The Mother Knot.* New York: McGraw-Hill, 1976; Durham, NC: Duke University Press Books, 1997.

Lebowitz, Fran. "Why not have your first baby at sixty, when your husband is already dead and your career is over? Then you can really devote yourself to it," in *Redbook.* Chicago, IL: Hearst Magazines, 1990.

Livingston, Gretchen. "Childlessness Falls, Family Size Grows Among Highly Educated Women." May 7, 2015. Accessed May 2018, http://www.pewsocialtrends.org/2015/05/07/childlessness-falls-family-size-grows-among-highly-educated-women/.

Midler, Bette. "Being a mother basically killed my ambition. I don't feel like someone is going to take [everything I've worked for] away. And I have this life that I love so much," on *Showbiz Today Show,* in *Ladies' Home Journal.* Iowa: Meredith Corporation, December 1998.

Organisation for Economic Cooperation and Development. "Family Database." Accessed August 2017, http://stats.oecd.org/Index.aspx?DataSetCode=FAMILY.

Parker, Kim. Pew Research Center. "Despite Progress, Women Still Bear Heavier Load Than Men In Balancing Work and Family." March 10, 2015. Accessed October 2017, http://www.pewresearch.org/fact-tank/2015/03/10/women-still-bear-heavier-load-than-men-balancing-work-family/.

Wang, Wendy. "Parents' Time with Kids More Rewarding Than Paid Work-and More Exhausting" Accessed October 2017, http://www.pewsocialtrends.org/2013/10/08/parents-time-with-kids-more-rewarding-than-paid-work-and-more-exhausting/.

Chapter Five

Coleridge, Samuel Taylor. in Alexandra Towle in *Mothers: A Celebration in Prose, Poetry, and Photographs of Mothers and Motherhood*. New York, NY: Simon and Schuster: 1988.

Diana, Princess of Wales. "If men had babies, they would only ever have one each," in *The Observer*, London, UK: Guardian Media Group, 1984.

Government of Canada."Pregnancy and Women's Mental Health in Canada." Accessed June 2018, https://www.canada.ca/en/public-health/services/publications/healthy-living/pregnancy-women-mental-health-canada.html.

Emecheta, Buchi. *The Joys of Motherhood*. London, UK: Allison and Busby, 1979.

Lamott, Anne. *Operating Instructions: A Journal of My Son's First Year*. New York, NY: Fawcett Columbine, 1994.

Marston, William Moulton (creator). *Wonder Woman*. TV series. ABC. 1975-1979.

Newport, Frank. Gallup News. "Americans Prefer Boys to Girls, Just as They Did in 1941." June 23, 2011. Accessed October 2017, http://news.gallup.com/poll/148187/americans-prefer-boys-girls-1941.aspx.

Priestley, JB. "To show a child what has once delighted you, To find the child's delight added to your own, So that there is now double delight seen in the glow of trust and affection...This is happiness," in *Reader's Digest*. New York, NY: Trusted Media Brands, March 1992.

Public Health Agency of Canada. "Results from the Canadian Maternity Experiences Survey." October 9, 2014. Accessed June 2018, https://www.canada.ca/en/public-health/services/publications/healthy-living/pregnancy-women-mental-health-canada.html.

Seager, Joni. "Not only do men generally want more children than women, virtually everywhere they typically dominate reproductive decisions," in *The State of Women in the World Atlas*. 2nd ed. New York, NY: Penguin Books, 1997.

Chapter Six

Adoption Council of Canada. "Myths and Realities." Accessed October 2017, http://www.adoption.ca/myths-and-realities.

Fey, Imogene. "A man finds out what is meant by a spitting image when he tries to feed cereal to his infant," chosen by Jilly Cooper and Tom Hartman, *Violets and Vinegar and Anthology of Women's Writings and Sayings*. London, UK: George Allen & Unwin, 1980.

Harris, Susan. (created by) *The Golden Girls*. TV series. IMDB.com, Accessed June 2018, https://www.imdb.com/title/tt0088526/quotes. 1985-1992.

Hawn, Goldie, Accessed October 2017, A to Z Quotes.

Herold, Don. *There Ought to be a Law*. New York, NY: E.P. Dutton & Company, 1926.

Higuchi, Shigekazu, Yuki Nagafuchi, Sang-il Lee, Tesuo Harada, "Influence of Light at Night on Melatonin Suppression in Children," September 1, 2014. *Journal of Clinical Endocrinology & Metabolism, Volume 99, Issue 9*. Accessed January 2018, https://academic.oup.com/jcem/article/99/9/3298/2538381.

Ladies' Home Journal, Iowa: Meredith Corporation: September 1998.

Lamott, Anne. *Operating Instructions: A Journal of My Son's First Year*. New York, NY: Fawcett Columbine, 1994.

"Newborn Babies and Sleep—Tips for New Parents." American Sleep Association. Dec. 2, 2016. Accessed June 2018, https://www.sleepassociation.org/sleep-disorders-n/more-sleep-disorders/children-and-sleep/newborn-babies-sleep-tips-new-parents/.

Paul-Carson, Patricia. Adoption Council of Canada. "Employment Insurance Benefits for Adoptive Parents." September, 2011. Accessed October 2017, http://www.adoption.ca/myths-and-realities.

Reik, Theodor. The main quote chosen by Alexandra Towle in *Mothers: A Celebration in Prose, Poetry, and Photographs of Mothers and Motherhood.* New York, NY: Simon and Schuster: 1988.

Chapter Seven

American Dental Association, Accessed June, 2018, https://www.mouthhealthy.org/en/az-topics/b/baby-teeth.

American Academy of Pediatrics. October 2011. "SIDS and Other Sleep-Related Infant Deaths: Expansion of Recommendations for a Safe Infants Sleeping Environment." Accessed March 2018, http://pediatrics.aappublications.org/content/early/2011/10/12/peds.2011-2284.

Centers for Disease Control and Prevention. "Occurrence of Down syndrome in the United States." Accessed February 2018, https://www.cdc.gov/ncbddd/birthdefects/downsyndrome/data.html.

Cox, Marlene. in *Ladies' Home Journal,* Iowa: Meredith Corporation, 1943.

Freud, Sigmund. "Quote chosen by Alexandra Towle in *Mothers: A Celebration in Prose, Poetry, and Photographs of Mothers and Motherhood.* New York, NY: Simon and Schuster: 1988.

Hepburn, Katharine. *Me: Stories of My Life.* New York, NY: Ballantine Books, 1996.

La Bruyere, Jean de and Nicholas Rowe. *The Works of Mons. De La Bruyere: The Characters, of Manners of the Age.* Andesite Press, 2015.

Lang, Susan S. *Cornell Chronicle.* November 20, 1997. "Grown Children Often Have Radically Different Views of Mother/Child Closeness." Accessed September 2017, http://news.cornell.edu/stories/1997/11/older-moms-have-favorite-children-and-admit-it-says-cornell-gerontologist.

Livingston, Gretchen. Pew Research Center. May 4, 2018. "More than a Million Millennials are Becoming Moms Each Year" Accessed June 2018, http://www.pewresearch.org/fact-tank/2017/01/03/more-than-a-million -millennials-are-becoming-moms-each-year/.

National Institute of Health. "Progress in Reducing SIDS." Accessed June 2018, https://www1.nichd.nih.gov/sts/about/SIDS/ Pages/progress.aspx.

Rogers, Fred. May 1, 1969. "One of the first things a child learns in a healthy family is trust." Fred Rogers testifies to Senate committee on Communications in 1969. Accessed February 2018, https://www.youtube.com/watch?v=fKy7ljRrOAA.

Mcalpine, Fraser. BBC America, Anglophenia. "Emma Watson in Quotes to Live By." Accessed September 2017, http://www. bbcamerica.com/anglophenia/2015/04/25-emma-watson-quotes-to-live-by.

Mayo Clinic. "Infant and Toddler Health." Accessed June 2018, https://www.mayoclinic.org/healthy-lifestyle/ infant-and-toddler-health/expert-answers/tummy-time/faq-20057755.

"Your Child's First Visit." Canadian Dental Association, Accessed June 2018, https://www.cda-adc.ca/en/oral_health/cfyt/ dental_care_children/first_visit.asp.

Chapter Eight

Beasley, Mary C. "Motherhood—an accident, an occupation, or a career," chosen by Alexandra Towle in *Mothers: A Celebration in Prose, Poetry, and Photographs of Mothers and Motherhood.* New York, NY: Simon and Schuster: 1988.

Covey, Stephen, *The 7 Habits of Highly Effective People; 25th Anniversary Edition.* Missouri: Turtleback Books, 2013.

DeGeneres, Ellen. "Accept who you are. Unless you're a serial killer. Goodreads. Accessed June 2018, https://www. goodreads.com/quotes/515427-accept-who-you-are-unless-you-re-a-serial-killer.

Goulding Smith, Elinor. *The Complete Book of Absolutely Perfect Baby and Child Care.* New York, NY: Harcourt, Brace, 1957.

Rodkey, Geoff. Daddy Day Care. Film. Directed by Steve Carr. Sony Pictures Entertainment. May 2003.

Chapter Nine

Anderssen, Erin. "Seven Things To Know About Canada's New Parental Leave Benefits." The Globe and Mail. March 24, 2017. Updated May 4, 2017, https://www.theglobeandmail.com/life/parenting/mothers-day/federal-budget-2017-maternity-leave/article34414374/.

Blake, William. "A Cradle Song" 1793/1794 (partial poem). Chicago, IL: NTC Contemporary Publishing Company, 1998.

Cherry, Kendra. "The 4 Stages of Cognitive Development." Updated May 24, 2018, https://www.verywellmind.com/piagets-stages-of-cognitive-development-2795457.

Dion, Celine. "My mom's my idol. She's a wonderful mom who left her dreams to raise fourteen children," on *Larry King Live*, in *Ladies' Home Journal,* 1998.

"Employment Insurance Maternity and Parental Benefits." Government of Canada. Accessed June 2018, https://www.canada.ca/en/employment-social-development/programs/ei/ei-list/reports/maternity-parental.html#h2.1.

Family and Medical Leave Act. US Dept of Labor. Accessed June 2018, https://www.dol.gov/whd/fmla/?apartner=aarp.

Hoover, Herbert. "Children are our most valuable resource." The New York Times, Obituary, October 21, 1964.

Jones, Franklin P. "Love doesn't make the world go round. Love is what makes the ride worthwhile," in Maggio, Rosalie. *The New Beacon Book of Quotations by Women.* Boston: Beacon Press, 1998.

Kim, Susanna. "US is Only Industrialized Nation Without Paid Maternity Leave." ABC News. Updated May 6, 2015, https://abcnews.go.com/Business/us-industrialized-nation-paid-maternity-leave/story?id=30852419.

McLaughlin, Mignon. *The Second Neurotic's Notebook.* Indianapolis: Bobbs-Merrill, 1966.

"Of 41 Nations, Only US Lacks Paid Parental Leave." Pew Research Center. September 26, 2016. Accessed June 2018, http://www.pewresearch.org/ft_16-09-19_parental_leave/.

Voice and Agency Empowering Women and Girls for Shared Prosperity. Accessed June 2018, http://www.worldbank.org/content/dam/Worldbank/document/Gender/Voice_and_agency_LOWRES.pdf.

Young, Mark C. *Guinness World Records.* Vancouver, BC: Jim Pattison Group, 2017.

Chapter Ten

Beecher, Henry Ward. "You cannot teach a child to take care of himself unless you let him try and take care of himself. He will make mistakes; and out of these mistakes comes his wisdom," said in a sermon and chosen by Alexandra Towle in *Mothers: A Celebration in Prose, Poetry, and Photographs of Mothers and Motherhood.* New York, NY: Simon and Schuster: 1988

Fitzhugh, Louise. *Harriet the Spy.* New York, NY: Dell Publishing Co. Inc, 1964. Fourth Dell Publishing, 1969.

Leslie, Amy. *Amy Leslie at the Fair.* Chicago, IL: W.B. Conkey, 1893.

Pythagoras. "Choose always the way that seems the best, however rough it may be; custom will soon render it easy and agreeable," chosen by Alexandra Towle in *Mothers: A Celebration in Prose, Poetry, and Photographs of Mothers and Motherhood.* New York, NY: Simon and Schuster: 1988.

Samperi, Kate. "Before becoming a mother I had a hundred theories on how to bring up children. Now I have seven children and only one theory; love them especially when they least deserve to be loved," chosen by Alexandra Towle in *Mothers: A Celebration in Prose, Poetry, and Photographs of Mothers and Motherhood.* New York, NY: Simon and Schuster: 1988.

Serreau, Colin, James Orr, and Jim Cruickshank. Three Men and a Baby. Film. Directed by Leonard Nimoy. Los Angeles. Buena Vista Pictures. 1987.

Torregrossa, Richard. Fun Facts about Babies. Dell Publishing, 1997; Newer Kindle Version: New York, NY: Random House, 2008.

Weaver, Janelle. "Crying Women Turn Men Off." May 1, 2011. Scientific American Mind. Accessed June 2018, https://www.scientificamerican.com/article/crying-women-turn-men-off/.

Williams, Serena. "Tennis is a game, family is forever." Accessed June 2018, via Brainy Quote, https://www.brainyquote.com/quotes/serena_williams_170261.

Young, Mark C. *Guinness World Records.* Vancouver, BC: Jim Pattison Group, 2017.

YouTube, *ESPN, "Serena Williams.."* https://www.youtube.com/watch?v=fY-vrfTASwk.

Chapter Eleven

Cavoukian, Raffi, Quote in Goodreads. Accessed May 2018, https://www.goodreads.com/quotes/385259-love-for-children-is-the-enormous-untapped-power-that-can.

Davis, Mary GL. "...love them, feed them, discipline them and let them go free. You will have a lifelong good relationship," chosen by Alexandra Towle in *Mothers: A Celebration in Prose, Poetry, and Photographs of Mothers and Motherhood.* New York, NY: Simon and Schuster: 1988.

Fern, Fanny. *Caper Sauce: A Volume of Chit-Chat about Men, Women, and Things.* New York, NY: W. Carleton & Co., 1872.

"Heatstroke Deaths of Children in Vehicles." Updated June 4, 2018. http://noheatstroke.org/index.htm.

Hughes, John. Mr. Mom. Film. Performed by Michael Keaton. Directed by Stan Dragoti. Los Angeles, Twentieth Century Fox, 1983.

Lebowitz, Fran. *Social Studies*. New York, NY: Random House, 1981.

Tennyson, Alfred Lord. "Happy he with such a mother! faith in womankind beats with his blood, and trust in all things high comes easy to him, and though he trip and fall, He shall not blind his soul with clay," in Robert A Bertram. *A Dictionary of Poetical Illustrations: Specially Selected with View to the Needs of the Pulpit and Platform*. British Library, Historical Print Editions, 2011.

Wright, Steven. "I was born by Cesarean section, but you really can't tell... except that when I leave my house, I always go out the window." Jokes by Steven Wright. Accessed June 2018. http://www.wright-house.com/steven-wright/steven-wright-Kn.html

Chapter Twelve

Anonymous. "A mother's love is reflected in the joyful faces of her loved ones."

Bonaparte, Letizia Ramolino. "My opinion is that the future good or bad conduct of a child depends on its mother," Napoleon's mother chosen by Alexandra Towle in *Mothers: A Celebration in Prose, Poetry, and Photographs of Mothers and Motherhood*. New York, NY: Simon and Schuster, 1988.

Buscaglia, Leo F. *Love: What Life Is All About*. New York, NY: Ballantine Books, 1996.

Dunst, Carl J., Andrew Simkus, and Deborah W. Hamby. 2012. "Relationship Between Age of Onset and Frequency of Reading and Infants' and Toddlers' Early Language and Literacy Development" Center for Early Literacy Learning in *CELL Reviews*, Volume 5, Number 3. Accessed November 2017, http://earlyliteracylearning.org/cellreviews/cellreviews_v5_n3.pdf.

Geisel, Theodor Seuss. *Oh, The Places You'll Go.* New York: Random House: 1990

Kelly, Marguerite, and Elia Parsons. *The Mother's Almanac.* Missouri: Main Street Books, 1975.

Mundra, Radhika. Quote in Goodreads, Accessed March 2018, https://www.goodreads.com/quotes/tag/pure-soul.

Nordine, Michael. "Women Directed Just 16 Percent of Feature Films Last Year, According to Directors Guild of America's Inclusion Report." *Indie Wire.* Updated June 21, 2018, http://www.indiewire.com/2018/06/directors-guild-inclusion-report-2017-1201977377/.

Chapter Thirteen

American Academy of Pediatrics. October 2011. "SIDS and Other Sleep-Related Infant Deaths: Expansion of Recommendations for a Safe Infants Sleeping Environment." Accessed March 2018, http://pediatrics.aappublications.org/content/early/2011/10/12/peds.2011-2284.

Acknowledgments: This book is dedicated to M. Callam Ingram. I would like to thank all of the people who contributed to or supported the creation of this book, including those mothers who chose to do so anonymously. I would like to thank the following people in alphabetical order: Judith Anastasia, Aubrey Arnason, Haleigh Atwood, Tiffany Beebe, Sherri Berns, Carmen Berry, Suzanne Bolton, Beth Brandon, Brynn Chase, Laura Jane Conrad, Hannah Daley, Miranda Frigon, Adad Hannah, Amber Haynes, Daniel Ingram, Brian Irwin, Wendy Jane, Linda Lee, Kristen Lepionka, Holly Lorincz, Nancy Mizgala Lewis, Jefferson Mooney, Alison Myers, Ron Peterson, Dee-Dee Pincott, Madelyn Pugh Davis, Molly Niles Renshaw, Angelita "Angie" Roman, Alex Rose, Alison Schmelke, Linda Shekerdemian, Doralina Silander, Amanda Solinas, Janelle Spillett, Sally Steiner, Terra Tailleur, Mary Trokenberg, Stella Tzanidakis, Lyza Ulrych, Helen Van Wart, Samantha van Tol, Kati Urszuly, Sandy Watro, Kara Ward, Lindsey Welsh, Sheldon Walker, Emily Wickingstad.

INDEX

Certificate of First Year
of Motherhood Completed

Date: _____